STEPHANIE LASHFORD

The
Allergy Cookbook

Illustrated by
KETHRINE KNIGHT

ASHGROVE PRESS, BATH

First published in Great Britain in 1983 by
ASHGROVE PRESS LIMITED
26 Gay Street, Bath, Avon, BA1 2PD

ISBN 0 906798 28 0 (hardcover)
ISBN 0 906798 26 4 (paperback)

First published October 1983

Dedicated to
Charles and Elizabeth –
God bless

Typeset in Plantin by Ann Buchan (Typesetters)
Walton-on-Thames, Surrey
Printed and bound in Great Britain by
Biddles Limited, Guildford & Kings Lynn

Contents

KEY TO COLOUR PLATES

Cover

Christmas Cake
Raised Pork Pie
Bread & Butter Pudding
Tofu Quiche Lorraine
Pork Goulash
Smooth Liver Pate
Selection of Wholemeal Bread

Egg-free Section

Kedgeree
Home-made Faggots
Humus bi Tahina
(chick pea spread)
Horseradish Sauce
Honey & Fruit Scones

Corn-free Section

Tuna Pie
Lemon Squash
Pork Goulash
Printanière— Simple Salad
Florida Cocktail
Home-made Peanut Butter

White-flour free Section

Minestrone Soup
Wholemeal Pork Pie
Pizza
Home-made Mincemeat
Fresh Fruit in Yoghurt
Traditional Welsh Cakes

Milk-free Section

Pomello Marmelade
Bengal Chutney
Sunshine Chicken
Date & Walnut Loaf
Tofu & Avocado Dip
Selection of fresh vegetables

ACKNOWLEDGEMENTS

I would like to thank
Sylvaine Faugère, for help in keeping the house together.
Margaret Foster, for typing the book and turning it into into English
    at the same time
Peter Campbell, for help with technical details
Bess Jones, for helping and encouraging me
Anne and Roger Pierson, for help with preparing the food, and for
    producing the photographs

A NOTE ON FOOD ALLERGIES

What is a food allergy? While medical opinion as to the cause differs, there is general agreement that it is a reaction of the immune responses of the body to substances which, to most people, are harmless, but to those with a food sensitivity are treated as 'invaders'. My own definition of what takes place is this.

The pancreas is unable to absorb the enzymes in certain food and drink; this in turn affects the entire digestive tract, which creates toxins. The alarm is then sounded for the adrenal glands to produce adrenaline, cortisone and histamine. While they are fit and healthy they perform their task admirably; but over a period of time the adrenal glands atrophy and reach a stage where they are unable to produce the A.C.H. the body requires. An allergy reaction is the outcome. This inter-reaction takes place as the system moves through the three stages of the General Adaptation Syndrome: initial reaction, adaptation and exhaustion.

There are many ways of discovering food sensitivity. The one I have found simplest and most accurate is a pancreatic nerve/muscle reflex test that is painless and attractive to all, especially children.

Make no mistake: food allergy is a widespread and growing problem. My own experience over the last five years has shown me that the average age of food allergy sufferers has dropped sharply and includes many children. The enormity of what will happen to future generations, should present-day methods of additive-mad food manufacturing persist, is frightening.

'Convenience' foods often contain a variety of substances to which many are allergic. Just ask the parents of hyperactive children, who rarely have a moment's peace during the day and precious little sleep at night, or the parents of children with eczema or asthma, or migraine, or indeed those people with rheumatoid or osteo arthritis. In all these conditions and many others it is now being discovered that food sensitivity can play a crucial part.

Stephanie Lashford has produced an extremely valuable book and one that has long been wanted. While it cannot hope to cater for every sufferer from a food allergy, it is likely to help thousands of people with food sensitivity problems through the 'allergy jungle'.

Gwynne H. Davies N.D., M.N.T.O.S
Taunton, August 1983

INTRODUCTION

To have a confirmed food allergy may lead you to believe that you have something most extraordinary. It may leave you feeling very uncertain what to do next. The question you are then likely to ask yourself is "How do I go about changing my everyday eating habits to accommodate my allergy?"

Well, some allergies are more difficult than others to fit into existing everyday eating habits, but the point is that once you have decided upon a certain eating pattern you must stick to your régime and never falter. It must become a way of life, and if a situation arises where you find yourself offered only allergy foods, then say, "No, thank you, I'm not hungry", or explain, as tactfully as possible, the reason for your refusal. People may at first consider you a little awkward or cranky, but *your* health, not theirs, should be your major concern. In time, people will get used to you and come to accept the fact that if you eat a certain food or collection of foods you will suffer some kind of physical or mental discomfort.

It has been stated that food allergies are associated with mental and physical symptoms. Some of these are minor but others can be most alarming. As the symptoms can be imprecise and difficult to identify, it becomes a problem to identify the actual allergy. The mental and emotional symptoms that people may suffer include anxiety, depression, irritability, mental lethargy, confusion, hyperactivity, restlessness, an inability to concentrate and indifference. Some of the physical disorders that have been attributed to food allergies are hay fever, skin rashes, asthma, migraine, fatigue, aching of the joints, constipation, diarrhoea, hearing problems and acne. These are often symptoms people put up with uncomplainingly, but which with a carefully thought out diet would disappear; and I am sure the people concerned would lead fuller, fitter and healthier lives.

What has motivated me to write this book? I obtained a Certificate of Education from the Teacher Training Department of Radbrook College, Shrewsbury, in Home Economics, following which I taught, and still teach, in schools and at evening classes. During this time I have witnessed a sad lack of awareness on the part of many people of what they eat and how their eating habits may affect them personally. Through my own discovered food allergies I have come to understand the effects of food upon the individual and wish to pass on the benefits of my own personal knowledge and experience to others who have also, because of particular food allergies, been putting up with certain

1

health problems. In some case the problems are hardly minor, in that the whole pattern of that particular individual's physical, mental and emotional life has been drastically affected by long established, unchanging eating habits.

I feel very sad that some G.P.s do not seem to think it their province to get at the root of a person's problems and are often content just to treat symptoms. This is where being aware of your own particular allergy or allergies is very important, as what may in the beginning be something simply annoying can, if left, turn into something very unpleasant. So if you have a confirmed allergy to the foods I am going to deal with, you may feel safe and confident in using the recipies I have devised. The aim of this book is not to diagnose but to help those with a confirmed allergy to egg (the white or yolk), corn, white flour or milk towards a greater enjoyment of their food and to help them cope with their allergy or allergies more confidently.

If you feel you have a health problem that has not been helped by conventional methods I would say, "Try other avenues". The old saying is quite right: "Nothing ventured, nothing gained...."

General advice on eating habits

The need to be aware of what you are eating is something I cannot stress strongly enough. You may feel that you eat well. This is an ambiguous statement, for what is well to one person may be poorly to another. But I do not wish to lecture you on how much of each particular nutrient you need daily as this topic appears in so many of the articles I read on food and eating habits.

I want rather to promote the idea of eating to suit the individual, for we are all so different. I do not believe that one can print nutritional tables which suit everyone. Each person seems to me to be like an individual chemical reaction – what you put into that person in the way of daily food makes them react in a certain way. I therefore feel that it is vital that each person works out for his or herself a satisfactory eating programme to keep his or her body functioning normally.

and nutrition to do this I would advise you to seek the help of a food allergy specialist. In my case it was Mr. Gwynne H. Davies of Taunton.* Such a specialist can assist you in working out the most satisfactory eating pattern for you to adopt to enable you to promote and enjoy a healthy body.

* See *Useful people and addresses* p. 146

If you wish to go it alone, however, here is some general advice that may be of benefit to you:

1. Eat only wholemeal bread.
2. Eat only brown rice or wholemeal pasta.
3. Reduce your sugar consumption by 30-50% and change to raw cane sugar.
4. Reduce the fat in your diet by 30-50%
5. Take some exercise for 30 minutes twice a week, e.g. walking, swimming, yoga.

A Question of Fat

Fats have been discussed at great length in the western world for the past few years. The opinion has been voiced that butter causes all sorts of problems, also that vegetable fat is better for you than animal fat.

Well, my own feelings on this matter are that we can all reduce our fat consumption by 50% and have no nutritional problems whatsoever, and this includes all the fats you eat that are hidden in the manufactured foods you buy, along with the fat in meat, bacon, cheese, etc.

It is important to remember that all the fat foods we eat usually contain other important nutrients, usually Vitamin A and Vitamin D, and protein in cheese, meat and eggs. So it is my advice to you to reduce the amount of fat you buy. I keep my family of four to ½ lb (225 g) of butter plus ½ lb (225 g) of vegetable margarine per week. This includes all the baking I do along with the fat we spread on our bread. If we run out then I'm afraid it's just hard luck until I do my once-weekly shopping again. This way I can keep a mental note of their average weekly consumption. Try also to avoid too many fried foods. I use a non-stick frying pan for my frying so that I can get away with using only a minimum amount. There are so many alternative ways of making foods palatable that one should really only rarely use one's frying equipment. I bake fish in the oven using only 2-3 teaspoons of vegetable margarine to stop it sticking.

I must point out that I do not advocate you give up eating fat entirely, but simply make a conscious effort to reduce your family's consumption.

One further point to bear in mind is that you do need extra in the

3

winter, but only a little extra. This should not be an excuse to launch into a massive fry-up.

A Question of Salt

Although we need salt daily for our bodies to function properly, it is unnecessary to take the excessive amounts that some people commonly do. For when you take in large amounts of salt your body has to excrete the excess in order to maintain the correct balance and in so doing gives the kidneys extra work. Over a period of years this can give rise to problems, one of which can be high blood pressure.

Another point to bear in mind is that if you are cooking for a baby or young child you must not in the first year of life give your child salt, as your child's delicate kidneys will have difficulty in dealing with the extra load. Although the food you prepare may taste bland to you, it will be quite acceptable to the child.

You will observe that throughout the book I have reduced the use of salt to a minimum. This is because I firmly believe that its use is really only a question of habit and that given time you will never consider the use of added salt in your diet. If you are one of those unfortunate people who suffer from higher than normal blood presure, one practice which I feel would do you nothing but good would be to eliminate all *added* salt from your diet. Try replacing your usual salt (sodium chloride) by potassium chloride which can be found naturally in such foods as tomatoes and some fruits, and can be purchased commercially as a salt substitute. If you are being treated for very high blood pressure I would discuss the problem thoroughly with your G.P. before you change your diet, as some medicines given for high blood pressure have diuretics in them and may cause other side effects. As I advocate throughout the book, eat what comes naturally and your health should improve.

There are several salt substitutes now available which can be purchased from most health food shops. One of these, called ruthmol, can be used in cooking although it should be added *after* the cooking instead of before. It is used throughout this book.

A Question of Sugar

It has been said that as a nation we consume enormous amounts of sugar annually. Leading nutritionalists have also said that we can do without *all* the sugar we eat. I feel that to try and make everyone give up all their sugar would be foolhardy and so I say reduce your sugar intake by half. This is a more realistic aim.

It would also be most beneficial to change from using the highly refined variety to partially refined raw cane sugar which contains trace elements of a variety of minerals and a small amount of roughage. It may be less sweet, but it still enables the making of conventional products such as cakes, etc. There are many sugars available nowadays and I am sure many people become confused by the various choices offered. Be careful, however, as some of the dark sugars are highly refined and then dyed using a variety of additives.

The ones I would recommend are:

Muscovado
A dark sugar which is excellent for fruit cakes and gingerbread. However, it has a heavy texture and is not suitable for sponge cakes. The flavour is quite strong and so a little only is needed if used to sweeten.

Raw Cane Granulated
Ideal for everyday use. It is versatile and can be made into:

    (a) *Caster Sugar* Simply grind for 1 minute in a grinder. Prepare a batch at one time and store.

    (b) *Icing Sugar* Grind for 3-4 minutes until you have a fine powder. Prepare it as you need it as it does not store very well. It gives a brown colour to meringues and icing but this does not detract from the flavour.

There is also a demerara variety available which is very useful in the kitchen.

Fructose
This is the sugar found in a variety of fruits. It is much sweeter than cane or beet sugar (approximately 1½-2 times sweeter) and so you need less of it. An added bonus is that it is less harmful to the teeth and so the risk of dental caries is reduced. Although expensive, it is a welcome addition to any cook's food cupboard. It is also suitable for diabetics but they should consult their G.P. before starting to use it. It can be used in many ways in baking, e.g. the wholemeal chocolate biscuit recipe in the book (*see* p. 135,) has fructose as an alternative to ordinary sugar.

Jaggery   *see* Glossary of Products Available, p. 146.
Maple Sugar   *see* Glossary of Products Available, p. 146.

A Question of Flour

Again a subject in itself. It is important to know the difference between the following:

a) *Wholemeal* – this is where all of the grain is used. It is the best type for bread making.

b) *81%-85% Extraction* is the same as wholemeal, except that some of the bran has been removed, so giving a finer flour to make cakes and pastry with. Sometimes called *wholewheat*.

If you want an even finer flour then simply sieve wholemeal, but you must remember you will be missing out on that all important roughage.

Baking Powder
As most baking powders have some added white flour it is important for those who wish to avoid white flour to read the labels carefully. I know for certain that *Sainsbury's* own and *Foodwatch* baking powder do not contain any white flour, but I cannot speak for any others.

Cookery Terms

Bain Marie
A large open dish (usually a roasting tin) half filled with water where such foods as pâtés and custards are baked to ensure that they remain below boiling point so that they do not curdle, burn or reduce in quantity during the required cooking time.

Baking Blind
A pastry case is cooked for 5-10 minutes before a filling is added, to ensure that the pastry is crisp and not tough.

Bouquet Garni
A collection of herbs usually tied in muslin to enhance the flavour of a dish. The herbs usually used are parsley stalks, a bay leaf, 2 blades of mace and 3 peppercorns.

Developing of flavour
To marinate leave mixture of ingredients in a cool place so that strong flavours of herbs and sauces are passed over to other ingredients.

Forcing bag
Or piping bag. Usually made of nylon and used to pipe cream, potatoes etc. Bigger than an icing bag.

Ramekin
Small china dishes of about ¼ pint capacity, originally from France.

To reduce
This means to simmer with the lid off to remove excess liquid, so that no thickening agents need be added.

Roux
A method of sauce making, using equal quantities of fat to flour. The sauce may be white or brown depending on how long you cook the mixture.

Spoons as a measure
They are all level unless otherwise stated.

Stock Making
Really a subject all of its own. I use mainly vegetable stock. Whenever I cook any vegetables I simply place the liquid in plastic containers in the deep freeze, and whenever I need stock I simply defrost all I require. If you want smaller quantities for children's meals place the stock in ice-cube trays.

You can do the same with any meat stock you have. It may be frozen with the risk of losing nutrients but it is always better than tap water and will last 3 months in your freezer.

Terrine
Is an oven proof dish, usually has a lid, often square and can be made from coated cast iron or earthenware. Used to make pâté in.

EGG-FREE RECIPES

The symptoms of an egg allergy are many. However, my only personal experience of someone with an egg allergy was our Nanny who I am sure was at the time heaven sent. I was due to go back to work as a school teacher after the birth of my daughter Suzanna and needed someone reliable and with a heart of gold to come into our totally disorganised household to look after my two children. I advertised in the local paper and although we had several replies I knew as soon as I met Nanny Knight that she was just the ticket.

The time came for me to return to school and Nanny Knight took charge, whereupon my every dream came true – two beautiful clean children, lots of clean smelling nappies, not to mention a tidy and orderly nursery.

You may ask – where does all this lead? It leads on to the summer months and Nanny arrives in the morning in a pretty summer dress, immaculate as always, but poor soul covered in enormous boils – covered, in fact from head to foot ... and this the result of eating eggs! It took a couple of weeks of very careful eating to get her skin back to normal. So if you are one of those unfortunate people who suffers such perverse effects from eating eggs then please take in all you can from the following chapter on a diet without eggs.

If you are trying to find out by yourself what you are allergic to by an elimination process then I would ask you to bear in mind that if you are allergic to the yolk you may not be allergic to the white, and vice versa, as their composition is very different and each may have an entirely different effect on you personally.

As an egg is a valuable source of a variety of nutrients which include protein, fats, vitamins A, B and D, iron, calcium etc., then it is important for you to try and replace them in your diet from other sources. The most obvious choices are red and white meat to replace the protein and B vitamins and vegetable margarines to substitute for the vitamins A and D. Quite simple to start with, but then you will have to start on an elimination programme which means you will have to read all the labelled ingredients very carefully on packeted foods.

Another point to bear in mind is that measles vaccine is grown in chick embryos; if your child or children are allergic to egg you may wish to discuss the matter with your G.P. before having your offspring vaccinated against measles.

Egg-free – A week's planned menu

	Breakfast	Lunch	Tea/Supper
Monday	Cleansing breakfast: juice of 1 lemon in a glass of warm water 1 bowl of muesli fresh fruit juice	Salad Platter and roast ham wholemeal bread and butter	Beef and Tomato casserole Green salad fresh fruit
Tuesday	2 rashers of grilled bacon grilled tomato wholemeal bread fresh fruit juice	Smooth Liver Pâté wholemeal bread fresh fruit	Quick Sausage Kebabs Boiled brown rice Soya Fruit loaf
Wednesday	beans on toast fresh fruit juice	Smokey Bacon Soup wholemeal bread	Traditional French Escalopes A selection of boiled vegetables fresh fruit
Thursday	A bowl of muesli fresh fruit juice	Pâté of Vegetables wholemeal bread fresh fruit	Tofu Quiche Lorraine Green salad Gooseberry Sorbet
Friday	Muesli Porridge	Pâté Maison Lettuce, Tomatoes Wholemeal bread and butter fresh fruit	Kedgeree Welsh tea bread – buttered – headed Bara Brith in index
Saturday	half a grapefruit wholemeal toasted bread fresh juice	Salad Platter 8 ozs grilled meat e.g. steak, pork chops fresh fruit	Grandmother's liver and onion A selection of boiled vegetables Honey and fruit scones
Saturday **Sunday**	Muesli fresh fruit juice	Veal Casserole boiled potatoes a selection of boiled vegetables Apple Charlotte	bread and honey No bake Mocha squares Swiss tarts Juice/Tea

EGG-FREE RECIPES

Starters
1. Humus bi Tahina
   (chick pea spread)
2. Smokey Bacon Soup
3. Pâté of Vegetables
4. Smooth Liver Pâté
5. Terrine of Rabbit
6. Parsnip Soup

Main Courses
7. German Style Red Cabbage
8. Beef and Tomato Casserole
9. Traditional French
   Escalopes
10. Quick Sausage Kebabs
11. Tofu Quiche Lorraine
12. Veal Casserole
13. Grandmother's Liver and
    Onions
14. Salad Platter
15. Kedgeree
16. Home-made Faggots

Sweets
17. Gooseberry Sorbet
18. Apple Charlotte
19. No bake Mocha Squares
20. Yummie Chocolate Sauce
21. Candied Gingerbread buns
22. Honey and Fruit Scones
23. Swiss Tarts
24. Australian Crunchie
25. Bara Brith – Welsh Tea
    Bread
26. Soya Fruit Loaf
27. Halva cups

Miscellaneous
28. Horseradish Sauce
29. Muesli Porridge
30. Salad Dressings
31. Damson Spread
32. Banana Treats
33. Fresh Fruit Milkshakes

Starters

1. *Humus bi Tahina* ENGLISH NAME CHICK-PEA SPREAD

Ingredients:

½ lb (225 g) dried chick peas
  or 12 oz (350 g) can of chick peas
  drained and rinsed plus 6–12
  tablespoons of cold water
1 teasp. ruthmol

3 medium sized cloves of garlic
  – crushed
6 tablesp. lemon juice
5 oz (150 g) Tahina paste
  (crushed sesame seeds)

Method

1. If you wish to use dried peas start preparation the day before by soaking them in cold water for at least 12 hours.

2. Drain the peas and either pressure cook them for 40 minutes in a modest amount of water *or*
place them in a heavy pan, cover with water and bring to the boil and then simmer for 2–3 hours until they are very tender. Top up the water as needed.
N.B. Keep the cooking liquid as this may be needed later on.

3. Place the peas, garlic, ruthmol, lemon juice and Tahina paste in a liquidiser and blend until smooth. The paste should be thin enough to spread. If too thick add some of the retained cooking liquid until the desired consistency is obtained.
If you do not have a liquidiser, mash the ingredients, then beat vigorously, and finally press through a sieve. Check the consistency, adjusting it by adding some of the retained cooking liquid if necessary.

4. Serve either on a small side plate garnished with water cress or in a larger bowl so that guests can help themselves.

Pitta bread is the traditional accompaniment to humus, but crackers, French toast or a selection of fresh vegetables are a pleasant alternative.

2. *Smokey bacon Soup*

Serves 4

Ingredients:

6 oz (175 g) smoked bacon
8 oz (225 g) onions – sliced
1¼ lb (560 g) potatoes
1 pt (570 ml) vegetable stock
2 level tablesp. flour – either
    wheat or potato

¾ pt (425 ml) milk – cow's,
    goat's or soya
2 oz (50 g) butter or vegetable fat
ruthmol and pepper

Method

1.   Melt the fat in a large heavy saucepan, and fry the onions until soft – but *not* coloured.

2.   Peel the potatoes, dice and add to the saucepan, frying for a further 15 minutes.

3.   Add the stock and simmer for 15-20 minutes until the vegetables are tender.

4.   Liquidise the mixture – it will then become a purée. Season.

5.   *To thicken*: blend the flour with a little of the milk. Add to the purée, along with the remaining milk.

6.   Bring slowly to the boil and allow to simmer for 3-5 minutes.

7.   Meanwhile chop up the bacon and fry in the frying pan until crispy and golden.

8.   *To serve*:   (a) test the seasoning
                 (b) pour into warm bowls and top each one with an ample serving of bacon.

3. *Pâté of Vegetables*

Serves 4

Ingredients:

4 oz (110 g) vegetable margarine
4 oz (110 g) onions finely chopped
2 sticks celery – finely chopped
8 oz (225 g) mushrooms – finely
  chopped
2 cloves of garlic – crushed
2 level tablesp. wholemeal flour
2 teasp. lemon rind

1 tablesp. lemon juice
good pinch of ruthmol and
  black pepper
6 tablesp. double cream or
  substitute e.g. soya milk
2-4 Green olives – stuffed
with pimentos

Method

1.   Melt the margarine very slowly – otherwise it will go brown. Add the onion and garlic and cook, without browning, for 4–5 minutes.

2.   Combine the flour with the celery and mushrooms, add to the onion mixture, stirring all the time. Cook for a further 10 mins or until the vegetables are tender.

3.   Season, then leave to cool.

4.   Mash the ingredients until smooth, using a fork, or liquidise if you are in a hurry. Add the lemon juice, mash, then add the cream or soya milk.

5.   Put the pâté into ramekins and leave in the fridge for 2 hours.

To serve: place on a bed of lettuce garnished with slices of olive.

4. *Smooth Liver Pâté*

Serves 4-6

Ingredients:

8 oz (225 g) chicken livers
  (pig's liver will also do)
8 oz (225 g) smoked bacon
1 very large onion

1-2 cloves of garlic – crushed
2 tablesp. sherry
2 tablesp. soya milk or top
  of the milk

Method
1.   Peel and slice the onion.

2.   Chop the bacon into small pieces.

3.   Chop the liver.

4.   Place the onion, bacon and garlic, and liver in a frying pan and cook until tender, about 20 minutes. A frying pan with a lid is ideal as the steam cooks the food, ensuring that all the food is cooked without becoming brown.

5.   Cool, then liquidise. Add the sherry and milk to give enough liquid for the liquidiser to work; you can choose the consistency of the pate by giving it between 2-6 minutes.

6.   Turn into a serving dish (¾ pint (425 ml) size) and place in the fridge until required.

N.B. Do not make too far in advance – 4-6 hours only.
This pâté freezes very well – for up to 2 months.

Serve with: Toast
                   Fresh wholemeal bread
                   biscuits *or*
                   in sandwiches for a packed meal

5. *Terrine of Rabbit*

Serves 8-10

Ingredients:

1¼ lb (560 g) boned rabbit (Your butcher will perhaps do this for you. Ask him to keep the kidney as this can be added to the terrine)

1¼ lb (560 g) sausage meat
1 teaspoon ruthmol
a good pinch of black pepper
1 liqueur glass of brandy

1 medium or large sized terrine or pot casserole

Method

1.   Cut the rabbit into very small pieces and place in a bowl, add the brandy and leave overnight for the flavour to develop.

2.   Chop the kidney (taken from the rabbit) and mix with the sausage meat, then add the juice from the marinated rabbit meat and mix well.

3.   Mix in the black pepper and ruthmol.

4.   To complete put layers of the meat, alternating with the sausage meat and rabbit flesh, into the terrine.

5.   Bake in a moderate oven for 1½ hours at Gas Mark 3, 170°C, 325°F.

Store in the fridge and use within 3-5 days of making.
Serve with chunks of wholemeal bread.

6. *Parsnip Soup*

Ingredients:

1 very large parsnip
2 cloves of garlic – crushed
1 teaspoon curry powder
2 pints (1.1 litres) vegetable stock
a good pinch each of
    black pepper and ruthmol

1 medium onion – chopped
2 oz (50 g) vegetable margarine
1 heaped tablespoon wholemeal
    flour
1 small carton natural yoghurt
chopped chives to garnish

Method

1. Trim the parsnip. Discard any damaged areas and then chop.

2. In a large heavy saucepan melt the vegetable margarine and add the parsnip, onion, garlic, black pepper and ruthmol. Cook very slowly for 10 minutes. Stir occasionally to prevent sticking.

3. Add the flour and curry powder. Stir well and cook for a further 2 minutes.

4. Slowly add the stock, bring to the boil and cook until the parsnip is tender.

5. Cool, then liquidise. Stir in the yoghurt and reheat gently. Do not boil.

6. Serve in warmed bowls and sprinkle with chopped chives.

Main Courses

7. *German Style Red Cabbage*

Serves 4-6

Ingredients:

1 medium red cabbage
(1¼-1¾ lb) (560-785 g)
1 oz (25 g) vegetable fat or oil
1 medium onion – chopped
5 tablesp. cider vinegar

4 tablesp. water
2 large cooking apples, peeled and
 grated
2 oz (50 g) raw cane sugar
1 oz (25 g) sultanas

Using a heavy tight lidded saucepan gives the best results

Method

1. Remove the outer leaves of the cabbage, slice very thinly, removing any hard stalks. Wash if necessary.

2. Heat the fat and add the onion and cook until soft.

3. Add the cabbage and stir well.

4. Add the vinegar and water. Bring to the boil and simmer for 20 minutes.

5. Add the grated apple and sugar to the cabbage and continue cooking for a further 10 minutes or until tender.

Place in a warmed serving bowl and sprinkle with the sultanas.
An excellent winter vegetable dish to warm and nourish the family at supper time.

8. *Beef and Tomato Casserole*

Serves 4

Ingredients:
1 lb (450 g) stewing or braising steak
2 tablesp. soya oil
ruthmol and black pepper
1 clove of garlic - crushed
herbs - basil, tarragon and parsley
 - a pinch of each,

1 lb (450 g) tomatoes - washed and
 quartered
4 oz (110 g) cooked haricot beans
½-¾ pt (275-425 ml) vegetable
 stock

Method
1.   Trim the meat and cut into cubes.

2.   Heat the oil and seal the meat. Add the garlic, ruthmol, black pepper and herbs.

3.   Add the stock, cover and simmer for 30-40 minutes.

4.   Add the tomatoes and haricot beans and stir gently.

5.   Place in the oven for 1 hour at Gas Mark 3, 170°C, 325°F. Remove the lid to allow the liquid to evaporate. Reduce so that there is sufficient liquid left to keep the meat moist, but not too much to flood the serving plates.

Serve with jacket potatoes, peas and cauliflower.

9. *Traditional French Escalopes*

Serves 4

Ingredients:
oil for frying

4-5-6 oz (110-150-175 g)
 veal escalopes

6 oz (175 g) breadcrumbs made
 from wholemeal bread
1 bunch parsley

Sauce: 1 medium tin of tomato purée
         1 small fresh chili
         4 tablesp. oil (sunflower gives the best results)
Serve: with a combination of 1 lb (450 g) potatoes and ½ lb (225 g) carrots
         boiled and mashed together to give colour to the completed dish,
         placed around the edge of the serving plate.

19

Method

1.   Prepare the sauce by trimming the chili, chopping it finely and adding it to the tomato purée and oil. Mix well. Put to one side.

2.   Take the veal and flatten it by using a steak hammer. Spread the sauce on each side, using all of it up.

3.   Dip the covered veal into the breadcrumbs.

4.   Shallow fry until cooked. This will take about 4-5 minutes each side.

5.   Peel and boil the potatoes and carrots until tender and mash until very smooth. A little vegetable margarine may be added, also a pinch of nutmeg improves the flavour.

To serve: Place the vegetable mixture on the serving plate and arrange the escalopes down the middle. Sprinkle liberally with the washed and chopped parsley.

10. *Quick Sausage Kebabs*

Serves 4

Ingredients:

1 lb (450 g) 100% beef sausages
1 small can pineapples – drained
1 large green pepper – trimmed
1 medium onion – peeled
4 large tomatoes

3 tablesp. Hoi-Sin sauce
   (or barbecue sauce)
2-3 oz (50-75 g) cooked boiled
   brown rice per person
8 kebab skewers

Method

1.   Cut the sausages into 3 equal pieces.

2.   Cut the pineapple, pepper and onion into cubes to make similar sizes to the sausages.

3.   Cut the tomatoes into quarters.

4.   Thread the ingredients onto the skewers evenly, ensuring that each one is the same.

5.   Spread the sausages with barbecue sauce.

6.   Either grill or cook on a charcoal barbecue.

7.   Serve on a bed of rice.

Quick and tasty for a mid-week supper dish. A good idea for a teenager's birthday party.

11. *Tofu Quiche Lorraine*

Makes 8 portions

Ingredients:

10¼ oz (285 g) Tofu
8 oz (225 g) animal rennet-free cheese
8 oz (225 g) smoked bacon
   – diced

2 large onions – peeled
   and sliced
black pepper
oregano

21

Pastry:

7 oz (200 g) wholemeal flour   2 oz (50 g) vegetable margarine
1 oz (25 g) cornflour   2 oz (50 g) vegetable fat
pinch of ruthmol   enough cold water to mix
A flan dish measuring 10″ (25 cm) in diameter
(Reduce the above quantities if you wish to make a smaller quiche)

Method

1. *To prepare the pastry*:
    (a) Mix the flour and cornflour together
    (b) Rub in the fat so that it resembles breadcrumbs.
    (c) Add enough cold water to mix to a dough. Use a
    rounded knife.

The rule for pastry is: 1 teaspoon of water to every ounce of flour.

2. Line the flan dish and bake blind for 10 minutes.

3. In a large bowl beat the Tofu with a fork until smooth. Add the
cheese – grated. Then add the onion and bacon which should be fried
for 10 minutes beforehand, seasoning with the black pepper and
ruthmol. Mix well and pour into the practically baked pastry case.
Sprinkle with oregano.

4. Place on the middle shelf of the oven for 45 minutes until golden
brown at Gas Mark 5, 190°C, 375°F.

Serve either hot or cold
with Salad
Coleslaw
Jacket Potatoes

N.B. This quiche does not freeze very well.

12. *Veal Casserole*

Serves 4

Ingredients:

1 lb (450 g) pie veal – cubed   2 teasp. tomato purée
1 large onion   ½ pt (275 ml) vegetable stock
¾ lb (350 g) tomatoes   1 teasp. raw cane sugar
pinch of ruthmol   2 bay leaves
¼ teasp. pepper   pinch of grated nutmeg
1 teasp. paprika   4 oz (110 g) soured cream *or*
1 medium pepper   natural yoghurt
   (red or green)   1 tablesp. oil

Method

1. Slice the onions, peel and slice the tomatoes.

2. Use the ruthmol and pepper to season the meat which has been cubed.

3. Prepare and slice the pepper.

4. Heat the oil, cook the onions for 2-3 minutes, then add the paprika and meat and cook for 3-4 minutes.

5. Stir in the tomato purée, tomatoes, pepper, stock, sugar, nutmeg and bay leaf.

6. Bring to the boil, cover and place in a moderate oven at Gas Mark 4, 180°C, 350°F for 1-1½ hours or until the meat is tender.

To serve: Top with the cream or yoghurt.

13. *Grandmother's Liver and Onions*

Serves 4

Ingredients:
1 lb (450 g) lamb's liver
2 lb (900 g) onions
cornflour and water paste:

1 tablesp. vegetable oil
¼ pt (150 ml) water

2 heaped teaspoons of cornflour
dissolved in ¼ tea cup of water

Method

1. Wash and trim liver. Cut the liver into thin strips ¼" x 3" (5 mm x 7.5 cm)

2. Peel the onions and slice thinly.

3. Using a large frying pan heat the oil and stir fry the liver for 2-3 minutes.

4. Then place the onion on top and add a quarter pint of water, cover and cook for 30 minutes until the meat is cooked and the onions are tender.

5. Thicken using the cornflour and water paste.

Serve straight away with freshly boiled potatoes and slices of wholemeal bread.
Simple, nutritious and economical.

23

14. *Salad Platter*

Serves 3-4

Ingredients:

8 oz (225 g) cooked, diced potatoes (in their jackets for extra vitamins!)
8 oz (225 g) cooked beetroot – diced
1 small fresh onion – peeled and diced

1 green pepper – prepared and diced
1 orange – peeled and diced
1 bulb of fresh chicory – shredded
pinch of dill seed
parsley to garnish

Dressing: olive oil and wine vinegar (6 tablespoons of olive oil and 3 tablespoons of wine vinegar); pinches of basil, parsley, ground cloves all mixed together well.

Method

1. Take a large platter, or a square plate.

2. Place the diced potatoes down the middle.

3. Place the diced beetroot down the sides.

4. Combine the tomatoes and onion together, add a pinch of dill seed and then place on each side of the beetroot.

5. Combine the diced pepper and orange together and place evenly on each side of the tomatoes and onion.

6. Finally add a layer of the shredded chicory to complete the platter.

7. Combine the dressing ingredients, shake and then pour over the salad.

Sprinkle with parsley and serve immediately.

A meal in itself – a mouth-watering combination of flavours to satisfy the most demanding of palates.

15. *Kedgeree*

Serves 3-4

Ingredients:

6 oz (175 g) long grain brown rice
¾-1 lb (350-450 g) of cooked fish –
  preferably a mixture of white
  and smoked e.g. smoked mackerel,
  cod, hake, coley
1 oz (25 g) butter or vegetable fat

1 tablesp. chopped parsley
1 teasp. ruthmol
1 teasp. pepper
½ lemon – cut into wedges
4 slices of wholemeal bread
  and butter

Method

1.   Cook the rice in ample water in a saucepan with the lid off (brown rice does take rather longer to cook, but is well worth the effort). Add 10-15 minutes extra to the cooking time for ordinary rice.

2.   Trim the fish, remove the skin and bones and flake into bite size pieces.

3.   Melt the fat in a large saucepan, add the rice and fish and toss until coated and thoroughly heated. Add the ruthmol and pepper.

4.   Turn into a warmed serving dish and garnish with the chopped parsley and lemon wedges.

5.   Cut the wholemeal bread and butter into triangles and serve on a separate plate.

A very nutritious supper dish that is both tasty and economical.

16. *Home-made Faggots*

Serves 4

Ingredients:

1 lb (450 g) wholemeal bread
  soaked in water
1 lb (450 g) pig's liver – liquidised
6 oz (175 g) bacon, streaky – liquidised

2 medium onions – liquidized
½ teaspoon dried sage
pinch of dried thyme

Method

1. You should use enough water to make the bread wet but not soggy. Beat with a fork to remove any lumps.

2. Liquidise the liver and bacon and onion. Chop the bacon and onion first.

3. Combine the bread and liquidised meat. Mix well using a spoon. Add the herbs, mix well.

4. Form the mixture into balls and place close together in a baking tin.

5. Bake in a hot oven at Gas Mark 6, 200°C, 400°F for 40 minutes until brown.

Serve with mashed potatoes and mashed swede.

Delicious on a cold winter's day.

N.B. Gravy can be served with meal made from
$\frac{1}{2}$ pint (275 ml) water
1 tablesp. cornflour
2 tablesp. soy sauce
1 teaspoon marmite

Blend together and bring to the boil.

Sweets

17. *Gooseberry Sorbet*

Serves 4

Ingredients:
½ lb (225 g) raw cane sugar
½ pt (275 ml) water
1 lemon rind peeled into strips
juice of 1 lemon

½ pt (275 ml) gooseberry purée
flavoured with a sprig of
elderflower

Method

1.   Dissolve the sugar in the water along with the lemon rind. When dissolved bring to the boil and boil for 10 minutes.

2.   Add the lemon juice and strain. Allow to cool.

3.   Add the fruit purée (seeds should be removed if a smooth sorbet is required). Mix thoroughly.

4.   Place in a rigid container and freeze.

To serve: spoon into chilled sundae dishes and garnish with two washed and sugared mint leaves.

18. *Apple Charlotte*

Serves 4

Ingredients:
1 lb (450 g) cooking apples
4 oz (110 g) raw cane sugar
3 oz (75 g) wholemeal breadcrumbs

1½ oz (40 g) vegetable margarine
rind and juice of 1 lemon

Method
1.   Peel and slice the apples *thinly*. Stand in water so they do not become brown.

2.   Mix the sugar, breadcrumbs and the rind of the lemon together.

3.   Drain the water from the apples and mix the lemon juice with the apple.

4.   Take an oven-proof dish and grease it. Then place half the bread crumbs in the bottom, then the apple slices and top with the remainder of the breadcrumbs.

5.   Melt the vegetable margarine and pour on the top.

6.   Bake in a moderate oven at Gas Mark 4, 160° C, 350° F for 30-40 minutes.

19. *No bake Mocha Squares*

Makes 9

Ingredients:
6-7 oz (175-200 g) shortcake-type
   biscuits (check the ingredients of
   the biscuits to ensure no
   egg has been added)
Topping:
2 oz (50 g) vegetable margarine
4 oz (110 g) raw cane icing sugar
2 level teasp. instant coffee
2 level teasp. boiling water

4 oz (110 g) vegetable margarine
2 level tablesp. golden syrup
2 oz (50 g) raw cane icing sugar

Method

1. Brush the base and sides of a shallow tin measuring 8″ square with oil.

2. Crush the biscuits in a paper bag with a rolling pin.

3. Break up the chocolate and place in a bowl over a pan of hot, not boiling, water until melted.

4. Add the fat, golden syrup and icing sugar and stir until dissolved.

5. Stir in the crushed biscuits.

6. Press the mixture into the prepared tin, level the top and leave to set.

Topping:

1. Cream the fat and sugar together.

2. Dissolve the coffee in the boiling water, and beat gradually into the fat and sugar mixture.

3. Spread evenly over the mixture in the tin. Place in the fridge until firm.

4. Using a sharp knife cut into squares.
Store in a tin.

20. *Yummie Chocolate Sauce*

Serves 4-6

Ingredients:
2 tablesp. water
2 tablesp. cocoa powder or carob powder
2 tablesp. syrup – cane or maple syrup

Method

1. Place all the ingredients in a small saucepan.

2. Heat gently until the ingredients are thoroughly mixed.

3. Allow to cool slightly and pour into a container if the sauce is not to be used immediately.

This will keep for 3-4 weeks covered in the fridge and can be used as a sauce or topping.

21. *Candied Gingerbread Buns*

Makes 10-12 buns

Ingredients:

8 oz (225 g) wholemeal flour
1 teasp. baking powder
½ teasp. bicarbonate of soda
4 oz (110 g) vegetable margarine
    or butter
4 oz (110 g) raw cane sugar
2 oz (50 g) candied peel

2 tablesp. maple syrup or molasses
3 tablesp. milk (soya, cow's or
    goat's)
1 teasp. ground ginger
½ teasp. mixed spice
2 oz (50 g) flaked almonds

Method

1.   Sieve the flour, baking powder, ground ginger, bicarbonate of soda and mixed spice together in a large mixing bowl.

2.   Melt the fat, sugar, syrup or molasses, stirring all the time. Ensure the mixture does not boil as this will spoil the texture of the buns.

3.   Add to the dry ingredients and mix using a metal spoon.

4.   Add the candied peel, along with the milk to make a consistency stiff enough to handle.

5.   With a little flour roll into even sized balls, and place on a greased baking sheet. Flatten slightly and sprinkle a few almond pieces on top.

6.   Bake for 15-20 minutes in the middle of the oven at Gas Mark 4, 180°C, 350°F.

7.   Cool on a wire rack.

Excellent for packed meals and picnics.

22. *Honey and Fruit Scones*

Makes 6 scones

Ingredients:
8 oz (225 g) wholemeal flour and
2 level teaspoons of
baking powder
pinch of ruthmol
1 oz (25 g) vegetable margarine

1 oz (25 g) raw cane sugar or
½ oz (10 g) fructose
2 oz (50 g) chopped raisins
1 tablesp. clear honey
¼ pt (150 ml) milk – cow's,
    goat's or soya

Method
1.   Mix the flour, ruthmol and baking powder together.
2.   Rub in the fat and then stir in the sugar and raisins.
3.   Place the honey on the dry ingredients and mix to a soft dough with the milk.
4.   Knead gently on a floured board to make the mixture smooth and using a crinkled cutter cut out the scone mixture into approximately six large scones.
5.   Place on a greased baking sheet and bake for 12-15 minutes at Gas Mark 7, 220°C, 425°F until well risen and golden brown.

To serve: Split and lightly butter.

23. *Swiss Tarts*

Makes 12

Ingredients:
4 oz (110 g) vegetable fat or butter
1 oz (25 g) caster sugar
2-3 drops pure vanilla

4 oz (110 g) flour – wheatmeal
icing sugar for dredging
raspberry jam or glacé cherries

31

Method

1. Cream the fat and sugar until light and fluffy, add the vanilla.

2. Fold in the sieved flour.

3. Using a piping (forcing) bag and a large star nozzle, pipe the mixture into paper cases, which have been put into pattie tins so that they will keep their shape.

4. Start at the centre of the bottom of each case and pipe with a spiral movement round the sides leaving a shallow depression in the centre.

5. Bake at Gas Mark 3-4, 180°C, 350°F, for 20-25 minutes.

6. When the tarts are cool fill the centres with jam or halved cherries.

To complete: dust with icing sugar

24. *Australian Crunchie*

Makes 10-12

Ingredients:

6 oz (175 g) vegetable margarine or butter
4 oz (110 g) wholemeal flour
4 oz (110 g) raw cane sugar

3 oz (75 g) desiccated coconut
1½ oz (40 g) cornflakes
  (if allergic use wheat flakes)
1 oz (25 g) cocoa or ½ oz carob powder

Method

1. Melt the fat.

2. Add the dry ingredients.

3. Press into a greased tin and bake in a moderate oven at Gas Mark 3, 180°C, 350°F, for 25-30 minutes.

4. Cut into squares and eat when cool.

Excellent for picnics and packed meals.

25. *Bara Brith* A TRADITIONAL WELSH TEA BREAD

Makes 1 loaf

Ingredients:
*1 cup – cold tea   *2 cups wholemeal flour
*1 cup – sultanas   2 teasp. baking powder
*1 cup raw cane sugar
   * Use the same cup throughout. An average sized tea-cup is required.

Method
1.   Soak the sultanas in the tea and sugar overnight.

2.   Mix in the flour thoroughly.

3.   Turn into a greased and lined loaf tin and bake at Gas Mark 3, 170°C, 325°F for one hour.

4.   Cool on a wire rack.

5.   Serve sliced and buttered.

This tea bread must be eaten within two days because it has no fat content, and so will dry out very quickly.

26. *Soya Fruit Loaf*

Ingredients:
*1 cup soya bran   * 1 cup mixed dried fruit
*1 cup goat's milk   * 1 cup wholemeal flour and
*1 cup raw cane demerara sugar   1 heaped teaspoon of baking
                                  powder mixed together very well

*Use the same sized cup throughout e.g. tea-cup

Method

1. Place the milk, dried fruit, raw cane sugar and soya bran in a mixing bowl.

2. Mix well and allow to stand for 30 minutes.

3. Line a 1-1½ lb (450-675 g) loaf tin with greaseproof paper.

4. Add the flour and mix thoroughly using a metal spoon.

5. Turn the mixture into the prepared loaf tin and bake at Gas Mark 4/5, 180°C, 350°F for 50-60 minutes until well risen and dark brown.

6. Allow to cool in the tin. Cover and eat the next day sliced and buttered.

---

27. *Halva Cups*

Serves 4

Ingredients:

8-10 oz (225-275 g) dark plain chocolate

4 oz (110 g) pistachio nut - halva

4 tablesp. sherry

4 oz (110 g) fresh raspberries

1 large fresh peach - skinned and chopped

1 small carton thick-set goat's yoghurt

8 fresh cherries with their stalks on

8 paper cake cases

Method

1. To prepare chocolate cups: melt the chocolate and pour enough into each paper case to cover, ensuring that the edges are neat. (Allow to set: this could be done the day before.) Remove the cases very carefully.

2. Into each case place ½ oz (10 g) of the halva and ½ tablespoon of the sherry. Allow to soak in.

3. Combine the chopped peach and the raspberries and then spoon carefully on top of the halva.

4. Spoon a little of the yoghurt on top and then carefully place the chery on top.

Chill before serving: two per person. Yummie!

Miscellaneous

28. Horseradish Sauce

Fresh horseradish is available in the autumn and to make your own using only pure ingredients will make your roast beef even more appetising.

Ingredients:

4 tablesp. horseradish
  (grated very finely)
*½ pt (278 ml) white sauce made from:
1 oz (25 g) vegetable fat
1 oz (25 g) flour

½ pt (275 ml) soya or goat's milk
pinch of ruthmol
1 tablesp. vinegar

Method

1. Wash and scrape the horseradish and grate into very fine flakes.

2. Beat the sauce well, add the seasoning, vinegar and horseradish.

3. Blend thoroughly.

4. Chill before serving.

The sauce may be frozen if you wish to make double quantities or have some left over. It will keep for up to 6 months.

* For Method for making white sauce, *see* recipe for *Boeuf aux champignons*, p. 49

29. *Muesli Porridge*

Serves 2-3

Ingredients:
*1 cup rolled oats – medium or coarse
*2½ cups water
2 oz (50 g) raisins
2 oz (50 g) sultanas
2 oz (50 g) chopped nuts (hazelnuts and almonds give the best flavour)

1-2 tablesp. bran
2 tablesp. clear honey
1 red dessert apple, cored
   and diced

* An average sized tea cup will do.

Method
1.   Prepare the oats as directed on the packet.

2.   Half way through the suggested cooking time add the raisins, sultanas and nuts. Stir well.

3.   When cooked add the bran, honey and apple.

4.   Serve straight away.

N.B. A little yoghurt or cream may be added. Stir it in well.

30. *Salad Dressings*

As most thickened dressings contain egg I feel that you should change to the French style of dressing which has a basis of oil, and wine or cider vinegar. Use one part of vinegar to 3 parts of oil, then add a selection of fresh and dried herbs to suit the type of salad being prepared.

Basic Vinaigrette Dressing

2 tablesp. vinegar	a pinch of the following:
8 tablesp. oil	basil, thyme, tarragon
	1 clove of crushed garlic

Method
Using a clean jam jar shake the oil and vinegar together and then add the herbs.

   This is to be used with a green salad.

Dressing for a fish salad:

1 tablesp. of lemon juice	1 clove of garlic – crushed
3 tablesp. oil	2 tablesp. parsley

Method
   As above.

Yoghurt dressing to serve with meat dishes e.g. Persian Lamb Kebabs

Ingredients:

¼ pt (150 ml) goat's milk natural yoghurt	4 mint leaves – washed and chopped
½ cucumber – diced	pinch of ruthmol
	¼ pt (150 ml) goat's milk

Method
1.   In a large serving bowl combine all the ingredients together.

2.   Chill thoroughly before serving.

31. *Damson Spread*

Ingredients:

3 lb (1.35 kg) ripe damsons son	14-16 oz (400-450 g) raw cane sugar
¼-½ pint (150-275 ml) water	to 1 lb (450 g) of pulp

Method

1.   Place the damsons in a saucepan with the water. Cover and cook very slowly until tender.

2.   Cool slightly then sieve the fruit, ensuring that you remove all the stones.

3.   Weigh the pulp – you should obtain approximately 2 lb (900 g) of pulp.

4.   Turn into a preserving pan and simmer until the pulp is thick.

5.   Add the sugar and continue cooking until quite thick.

6.   Pour into clean, hot jars and seal at once.

Store in a cool place and use within 6 weeks.

The yield should be between 3-3½ lb (1.35-1.6 kg) of damson spread – pure, wholesome goodness, free of chemical colourings and preservatives, which you can safely enjoy on your bread, scones, etc.

---

32. *Banana Treats*

This is a recipe given to me by a friend who comes from the West Indies. The banana treats are a way of using ripe bananas, and are usually eaten in the late afternoon to keep the family going until supper time.

Ingredients:

3-4 small very ripe bananas
enough wholemeal flour to
    make a soft, but firm dough

a little sugar may be added
    if desired

Method

1.   Mash the bananas in a bowl using a fork, until all the lumps have gone.

2.   Add enough wholemeal flour to make a soft but firm dough.

3.   Using a frying pan heat a little oil and using a wet tablespoon drop heaped tablespoons of the mixture into the oil. Cook for 2-3 minutes then turn and cook for a further 3 minutes.

4.   Place on a kitchen towel to absorb any excess oil and serve at once.

Delicious and a good idea for those hungry children coming home from school.

This makes approx 16 banana treats.

33. *Fresh Fruit Milkshakes*

It is vital that we have sufficient daily nutrients to ensure that our bodily functions are carried out correctly. As well as eating well balanced meals, we can also enjoy well balanced drinks, and a combination of milk and fruit is ideal. Milk and fruit give protein, calcium, Vitamins A, D and C and a selection of trace elements, which we need but in such small quantities that it is often difficult to name them all.

Ingredients:
1 pint of milk – cow's or goat's
fruits suitable to use:
(a) 1 banana, 2 fresh apricots
(b) 1 peach, 2 oz (50 g) raspberries
(c) 1 small apple, 2 oz (50 g) blackcurrants
(d) 6 oz (175 g) strawberries

Method
1.   Simply place the milk and the desired fruits in a liquidiser and blend for 3-4 minutes.

2.   Serve on crushed ice in tall glasses.

Although this type of milk shake may not be as sweet or as colourful as the commercial varieties you can be sure you are getting all those vital nutrients that you need, without any of the chemicals that are put into the commercial varieties.

My children are hooked on them and if you let children help you they will be even more interested. I am very pleased as I prefer them to know the real taste of food and fruits and not the taste of artificial flavours.

WHITE FLOUR-FREE RECIPES

White flour
It seems from my own investigations and discussions with other people over the past years that an allergy to white flour is indeed very common. It is also a saddening fact that this has only come about through social snobbery. It was only those people who had sufficient money who could afford to buy refined flour and those who were poor could only purchase flour that was unrefined. As time passed poorer people wanted to be like the 'rich' and so eventually everyone's ambition became to have white bread at their table.

This may have been one up on the social ladder but it became a step back as far as adequate nutrition was concerned, as people were losing out on the B vitamins and roughage, or fibre as we now tend to call it. Unfortunately, people were not then aware of this sad fact, and so the fashion and demand continued. The age of high refinement had begun. This new fashion in eating also coincided with the period covering the two world wars, in which farming became more intensified and the aim became to get as much out of the land as possible. Scientists decided in their wisdom to develop chemical or "unnatural" fertilisers, as I prefer to call them, which came into daily use. So there we have the sad story. I believe these steps to be the very beginning of the present day decline in the health of this nation.

Firstly, white refined flour came into daily use and secondly, because it could now be grown in large quantities ways had to be found of making it last – so back to the scientists. Well, how about adding a few chemical preservatives. Yes, they thought, excellent idea. Had they thought of, or even considered, any possible long-term effects. NO! And they certainly hadn't thought of me – as I am one of their victims. I am not allergic to the flour itself but to the chemicals or rather preservatives that are added to the flour. You may ask 'Why doesn't she just buy white flour without the preservatives?' Well, because of legislation it is not possible to do this. Strict rules govern the production of flour in this country; if you are sufficiently interested, there are several government white papers on this topic.

My main concerns are the additives in flour: not the chalk vitamins B etc. which are used to bring it back to the nutritional equivalent of wholemeal flour, but the additives, and unfortunately there are many. The one I am most concerned about is Benzoyl peroxide, which was once and may still be used in the curing of fibreglass.

Unfortunately, this is not the end of the story. The manufacturing industry has jumped hastily onto the preservative band wagon and now has a vast selection of foodstuffs available to them along with a wide range of preservatives to make food last longer. They are now able to make foodstuffs en masse, cramming them with preservatives, popping them into expensive but attractive packaging and charging us small fortunes for the privilege of becoming more unhealthy as time goes on.

A dramatic statement you may say, but you have only to look at medical statistics to give you some idea of the magnitude of the problem. Take one condition – obesity, or the malnutrition of affluence as I prefer to call it. This has never previously been known on the scale we have it today; indeed, in times gone past it was almost unheard of in younger people.

So if you wish to ensure that you stay away from the additives in flour, simply switch to wholemeal. There are many exciting ways of using it as you will see in the recipe book.

This is not the end of the story. The millers now wish to put preservatives into *all* flour, including wholemeal, just to improve its shelf life.

Is nothing safe?

White flour-free – A week's planned menu

	Breakfast	Lunch	Tea/Supper
Monday	Cleansing breakfast: juice of 1 lemon in a glass of warm water 1 bowl of muesli fresh fruit juice e.g. orange or grape	Pizza Salade Sylvaine	Boeuf aux champignons savoury rice Mixed fruit crumble Natural yoghurt
Tuesday	Tropical Muesli	Sorrel Soup wholemeal toast fresh fruit	Simple Duck Cassoulet Watercress and orange salad
Wednesday	2 slices of melon *or* 1 grapefruit with honey	Welsh Dragon Eggs lettuce and tomatoes fresh fruit in yoghurt	Dry Vegetable Curry brown rice fresh fruit
Thursday	Poached egg on wholemeal toast juice	Minestrone Soup wholemeal rolls fresh fruit yoghurt	Crabe au Pamplemousse Pineapple Up-side Down Pudding and yoghurt
Friday	Grapefruit with honey Juice	Home-made ¼ pounders (110 g) in a wholemeal roll french fried potatoes fresh fruit juice	Fish in golden crumbs lemon wedges Selection fresh vegetables grilled tomatoes fresh fruit salad
Saturday	Porridge with honey Juice	Minestrone Soup wholemeal bread fresh fruit Juice	Pork chops in a pepper and mustard sauce brown rice, sweetcorn fresh fruit
Sunday	Apricot and Walnut Muesli Juice	Rosemary's Roast Lamb Tomato boats, potatoes Mint sauce Apple and Honey pudding	Afternoon slices Chocolate fingers Scones and jam Home-made lemonade

WHITE FLOUR-FREE RECIPES

Starters
34. Minestrone Soup
35. Sorrel Soup
36. "Salade Sylyvaine"
37. Pâté Maison
38. Egg and Anchovy Starter
39. Marinated Mushrooms

Main Courses
40. Boeuf aux champignons
41. Dry Vegetable Curry
42. Quick Saturday Lunch
    (Pork Chops in Pepper
    and Mustard Sauce)
43. Pizza
44. Fish in Golden Crumbs
45. Simple Duck Cassoulet
46. Welsh Dragon Eggs
47. Crabe au Pamplemousse
48. Rosemary's Roast Lamb
49. Quick Tuna Supper
50. Home-made beefburgers –
    ¼ pounders (110 g)
51. Wholemeal Pork Pie
    (Hot water pastry)

Sweets
52. Scones
53. Wholemeal Chocolate Cake
54. Apple and Honey Pudding
55. Parsnip Loaf
56. Banana Tea Bread
57. Gingerbread
58. Afternoon Slices
59. Mixed Fruit Crumble
60. Victoria Sandwich Cake
61. Pineapple and Rye Up-side
    Down Pudding
62. Traditional Welsh Cakes
63. Chocolate Fingers
64. Fresh Fruit in Yoghurt

Miscellaneous
65. Candied Peel
66. Christmas Cake
67. Home-made Mincemeat
68. Wholemeal Salad Cream
69. Apricot and Sultana Cake
70. Bread Sauce

43

Starters

34. *Minestrone Soup*

Serves 4

Ingredients:

4 oz (110 g) dried haricot beans
   – cooked
1 large onion – diced
1 clove of garlic – crushed
2 carrots – diced
10 oz (275 g) tomatoes – fresh
   or tinned

half a small white cabbage
   – shredded
2½ pts (1.4 litres) water or stock
   (*See* stock making)
Good pinch ruthmol
1 teasp. oregano
2 oz (50 g) wholemeal macaroni
2 tablesp. vegetable oil

Method

1.   Fry the onion, carrots and garlic until golden.

2.   Add the stock and bring to the boil. Lower to simmer for two minutes.

3.   Add the tomatoes and cabbage along with a sprinkling of ruthmol and oregano.

4.   Simmer for ten minutes.

5.   Add macaroni and haricot beans and simmer until cooked (approx 15-20 mins).

Serve piping hot with a little grated cheese on top.

35. *Sorrel Soup*

Serves 4

Ingredients:

1 pt (570 ml) stock – vegetable or meat will do
1 pt milk (cow's or goat's)
*1 lb (450 g) sorrel
½ lb (225 g) boiled potatoes complete with skins

4 oz (110 g) carton sour cream and a dash of nutmeg
1 oz (25 g) vegetable margarine
4 egg yolks
ruthmol and pepper

*The sorrel should be fresh – if you grow your own so much the better

Method

1.   Wash the sorrel and pour boiling water over it. Drain and chop finely.

2.   Melt the margarine and cook the sorrel until tender.

3.   Rub through a sieve or liquidise.

4.   Mash the potatoes and add to the sorrel purée.

5.   Heat the stock, add the milk, bring to the boil.

6.   Add the sorrel mixture and seasoning.

7.   Simmer for 10 minutes, then remove from the heat.

8.   Mix the egg yolks with a little of the soup, then gradually add to the soup. This should slightly thicken the soup.

9.   Serve with a topping of soured cream and a dash of nutmeg.

36. *"Salade Sylvaine"* (for hors d'oeuvre)

Serves 4-6

Ingredients:
1 large ripe, but not brown,
    Avocado pear
2 William pears, ripe but not soft
Dressing:
1 carton natural yoghurt
(cow's or goat's)
1 teasp. olive, soya or
walnut oil
3 teasp. lemon juice

3-4 oz (75-110 g) ham
    – cut into small pieces
2 teaspoons lemon juice

pinch of paprika
pinch of black pepper
pinch of ruthmol

Garnish: A selection of large washed lettuce leaves (Cos lettuce is ideal).

Method
1.   Take the serving plates and place three lettuce leaves on each, with the ends trailing over the edges like fans.

2.   Prepare the dressing – pour the yoghurt into a bowl, add the oil and lemon juice and mix in with the paprika, black pepper and ruthmol.

3.   Peel the avocado and pears. Cover all the cut surfaces with lemon juice to inhibit the action of the enzymes which will otherwise turn the fruits brown. Chop into "bite size" pieces and put into the yoghurt mixture.

4.   Add the pieces of ham and mix thoroughly.

5.   Spoon the mixture carefully onto the beds of lettuce and place a pinch of paprika on top of each individual salad.

To serve: chill for 30 minutes in the fridge.
This is an excellent start to a meal where there are to be stronger-flavoured foods.

37. *Pâté Maison*

Serves the world and his wife!

Ingredients:
2 lb (900 g) boned rabbit
1 lb (450 g) streaky bacon – smoked
  can also be used
1 large onion
3 large cloves of garlic – crushed
A large terrine or pot casserole with a lid

3 tablesp. chopped fresh parsley
  and thyme (mixed)
1½ teasp. ruthmol
½ teasp. black pepper

Method
1. Mince the rabbit meat, onion and garlic and bacon – making it smooth in texture.

2. Add the ruthmol and pepper.

3. Sprinkle the parsley and thyme over the bottom of the terrine.

4. Add the minced meat mixture and smooth the top evenly all over.

5. Cook in a medium oven at Gas Mark 3, 170°C, 325°F for 1½-1¾ hours.

6. Cool and store in the fridge.

Serve each portion with crisp lettuce and a slice of buttered wholemeal bread or rye crisp bread.

38. *Egg and Anchovy Starter*

Serves 4

Ingredients:
4 hard boiled eggs, size 1 or 2
1 tablespoon tomato ketchup
2 oz (50 g) can anchovies
2 tablesp. natural goat's yoghurt

8 crisp, washed lettuce leaves
8 tomato wedges
½ teasp. chopped parsley

47

Method

1. Cut the eggs lengthwise. Remove the yolks and place in a small bowl.

2. Drain the anchovies and combine with the yolks. Pound them together until smooth and then stir in the tomato ketchup.

3. On individual plates place the lettuce leaves, then the egg whites and fill with the yolk mixture, using a teaspoon.

4. Garnish with the tomato wedges and a dash of chopped parsley on top of each egg.

A simple starter but a good way of eating eggs, which are a good source of body building protein.

39. *Marinated Mushrooms*

Serves 4

Ingredients:

¾ lb (350 g) button mushrooms
2 tablesp. lemon juice
2 cloves of garlic – crushed
¼ pt (150 ml) red wine
2 tablesp. soya oil

a good pinch each of black
    pepper and ruthmol
a pinch of the following herbs –
    parsley, basil, dill seed

Method

1. Wash the mushrooms and drain.

2. Crush the garlic and place in a bowl. Combine with all the other ingredients mixing well. Leave overnight for the flavours to mingle.

3. Place in an oven proof dish and bake at Gas Mark 6, 200° C, 400° F for 25 minutes.

4. Transfer into ramekins and serve with garlic bread.

An excellent starter that is simple but very tasty.

Main Courses

40. *Boeuf aux champignons*

Serves 4

Ingredients:

Meat Patties
1 lb (450 g) lean minced beef
3-4 oz (110 g) wholemeal breadcrumbs
1 egg
a pinch each of thyme and basil

Mushroom Sauce
½ lb (225 g) mushrooms – washed, not peeled
2 oz (50 g) butter or vegetable fat
½ pt (275 ml) soya, goat's or cow's milk

1 oz (25 g) wholemeal flour
seasoning – black pepper and ruthmol

Swiss Potatoes
2 lb (900 g) potatoes – boiled and diced
4 oz (110g) wholemeal bread-crumbs
1 oz (25 g) butter for frying)
black pepper

Method
1.   Mix minced beef, bread crumbs and herbs together and bind using the egg.

2.   Shape into beef burgers and put on a plate in the fridge for two hours. (These can be made the day before if you wish.)

3.   Take the potatoes which have been diced into even pieces approximately the size of a stock cube.

4.   Melt the fat for frying, add the potatoes and gently stir to prevent sticking. Add the bread crumbs and stir until the potatoes have an even coating. Sprinkle with black pepper. Once this is done place on a serving plate and put in a warm oven until required.

5.   Either grill or gently fry the beefburgers until done. Place down the centre of the serving dish and return to the oven whilst you prepare the sauce.

6.   In a medium saucepan (non-stick is best) melt the fat and fry the mushrooms. Remove the mushrooms from the saucepan and put onto a plate.

7. Put the flour in the saucepan with the remaining fat. to make a roux and blend in the milk gradually until no lumps remain. Bring slowly to the boil stirring all the time. Add seasoning and the mushrooms. Stir well.

8. Pour over the beefburgers to complete the dish.

Serve with a fresh green salad.

41. *Dry Vegetable Curry*

Serves 3-4

Ingredients:

½ lb (225 g) cauliflower
3 medium potatoes
2 medium onions
¼ lb (110 g) green beans
1 inch (2.5 cm) fresh ginger
2 tablesp. vegetable oil

½ teasp. ruthmol
2 tomatoes
¾ teasp. turmeric
½ teasp. chili powder
1 teasp. mustard seed
2 teasp. garam masala

Method

1. Cut and chop the vegetables into bite size pieces, wash and drain.

2. Fry the onions and ginger in the vegetable oil for two minutes.

3. Add the potatoes, cauliflower, beans and salt and continue to cook for a further two minutes.

4. Add the tomatoes, turmeric, chili and mustard seed.

5. Cover and cook until the vegetables are tender, but still retain some crispness.

6. Sprinkle on the garam masala. Reduce the heat and continue cooking until all the liquid disappears. Stir carefully to avoid breaking the vegetables.

7. Serve on a bed of boiled brown rice.

42. *Quick Saturday Lunch*
(Pork chops in pepper and mustard sauce)

Serves 4

Ingredients:

4 pork chops (remove excess fat)
1 oz (25 g) cornflour
½ pt (275 ml) stock or vegetable water
1 heaped tablesp. French mustard
   (the type with whole grains in)

2 teasp. honey – clear
1 small red pepper, diced
black pepper

Method

1.   Brown the pork chops and red pepper in a non stick frying pan. Place in a 2 pt (1.1 litre) oven proof dish.

2.   Put the stock into the frying pan and add the honey, mustard and black pepper.

3.   Mix the cornflour to a smooth paste with a little water and add to the stock mixture.

4.   Bring slowly to the boil and ensure the sauce is smooth.

5.   Pour the sauce over the chops and cover with foil or a lid.

6.   Place in the oven at Gas Mark 3, 170°C, 325°F, for ¾ hour, or until the chops are done.

Serve on a bed of Swiss Potatoes (*See* Page 49) or a crisp green salad.

51

43. *Pizza* (QUICK METHOD)

Ingredients:

10 oz (275 g) wholemeal flour   ¼ pint (150 ml) goat's milk,
1 teasp. baking powder   cow's milk or soya milk
1 oz (25 g) fat, vegetable fat or Vitaquell

Toppings

Italian -   1 oz (25 g) green peppers; 1 small tin of tomatoes; 1 oz (25 g) green olives; 2 oz (50 g) cheese (vegetarian); a sprinkling of oregano

Greek -   1 small tin of tomatoes; 1 oz (25 g) garlic sausage; 2 oz (50 g) cheese (vegetarian); garlic salt; 2 oz (50 g) red pepper

English -   1 small tin of tomatoes; 1 oz (25 g) bacon; 1 oz (25 g) mushrooms; 2oz (50 g) cheddar cheese (vegetarian); black pepper

Method

1. Put the flour in a bowl, add the baking powder and mix thoroughly.

2. Rub in the fat, add the liquid all at once and mix to a soft dough.

3. Place on a floured surface and knead gently until smooth.

4. This mixture will make either one large or two individual pizzas.

5. Roll out into a circle measuring ¼" (5 mm) in thickness.

6. Toppings – all topping ingredients should be washed and chopped into bite size pieces and placed on small plates. Always put the tomato on the pizza base first, chopped up so that there are no large lumps. Sprinkle all the other ingredients on evenly, leaving the cheese until last. Finish with the herbs.

7. Place on the middle shelf of an oven at Gas Mark 5, 180°C, 375°F for 25-30 minutes, or until the topping is cooked.

Serve hot with a crisp salad or a portion of coleslaw.

44. *Fish in Golden Crumbs*

To replace the prepared fish products to be found on the market containing many additives, colourings, etc., which detract from the succulent and delicate flavour of the fish, I suggest you try the following recipe to tempt your family when they want a fish supper.

Serves 3-4

Ingredients:
1 lb (450 g) fillets of any white fish, e.g. Cod, Haddock, Plaice, Coley
1 egg
4-6 oz (110-175 g) wholemeal bread – made into crumbs

black pepper
4 tablesp. oil; I personally would choose soya oil; vegetable would also do
lemon wedges

Method
1. Beat the egg and add the black pepper.
2. Place the bread crumbs on a plate.
3. Dip the fish fillets into the egg and then into the bread crumbs.
4. Repeat to ensure all the fish is covered.
5. Heat the oil and shallow fry gently for seven minutes each side. Drain on kitchen paper.

Use lemon wedges to decorate. Serve with sautée or french fried potatoes and a peas and sweetcorn mix.

45. *Simple Duck Cassoulet*

Serves 4-5

Ingredients:
1 medium onion – sliced
4 oz (110 g) streaky bacon – cut into pieces
2 level tablesp. wholemeal flour
1 15 oz (425 g) tin red kidney beans (drained)
1 15 oz (425 g) tin cannelloni beans (drained)
1 15 oz (425 ml) tin tomatoes

¾ pt (425 ml) vegetable stock
1 home made bouquet garni
½ lb (900 g) 100% beef sausages – cooked and sliced*
One small duck 2-2¼ lb (900 g-1 kg) roasted and cut into bite sized pieces)
ruthmol
black pepper

Method

1. Fry the onion and bacon together until soft and golden in a large casserole dish. No oil needs to be added as the fat from the bacon will prevent the onions from sticking.

2. Sprinkle on the flour and stir well (off the heat).

3. Add the beans (drained) and the tomatoes and mix gently.

4. Add the vegetable stock and bouquet garni, duck, and sausages and allow to come to the boil.

5. Season with ruthmol and black pepper.

6. Place in a moderate oven for forty minutes to heat through.

Serve with wholemeal bread rolls and a lettuce, watercress and spring onion salad.

A real winner to impress dinner guests!

*

46. *Welsh Dragon Eggs*

Serves 4

Ingredients:

1 lb (450 g) 100% beef sausages
1 small leek
1 tablesp. washed and chopped parsley
4 hard boiled eggs, size 4

1 beaten egg
6 oz (175 g) wholemeal bread-crumbs
ruthmol and black pepper

Garnish: lettuce and tomato wedges

Method

1. Remove the skins from the sausages and place the sausage meat in a bowl.

2. Trim and wash the leek and chop it very finely using a sharp knife.

3. Add the chopped parsley, ruthmol and black pepper, and prepared leek to the sausage meat and mix thoroughly using a fork.

4. Remove the shells from the boiled eggs and place in cold water.

5. Divide the sausage meat into 4 equal balls and flatten using wholemeal flour to prevent them sticking.

6.   Place an egg in the middle of the sausage meat and wrap the sausage meat around ensuring it is smooth with no cracks. Repeat with each egg.

7.   Roll each egg in the beaten egg and roll in the bread crumbs. Ensure all the egg is covered – repeat if necessary.

8.   Place on a baking tray and place in the oven at Gas Mark 4, 180°C, 350°F, for 40-50 minutes until cooked.

Cool before serving. Place on a bed of lettuce decorated with tomato wedges.

---

47. *Crabe au Pamplemousse* (CRAB WITH GRAPEFRUIT)

A succulent main dish that is delicate but interesting. It can be served as a starter if reduced in quantity but is also excellent to take as a special picnic lunch. The recipe below is for an individual portion, but may be altered accordingly.

Ingredients:

3-6 oz (75-175 g) dressed crab – white meat only (fresh is better, but tinned will do)
1 grapefruit, cut lengthwise in half

3 lettuce leaves – washed and shredded
2 tomatoes – cut into wedges

Dressing: the juice and pulp of half the grapefruit; 1 tablespoon of olive oil; 2 tablespoons of chopped parsley; ruthmol and pepper

Method

1.   Place the shredded lettuce on a serving plate.

2.   Place the dressed crab in the middle.

3.   Peel one lengthwise half of the grapefruit and arrange the pieces around the crab, along with the tomato wedges.

4.   *Dressing*:   combine the remaining grapefruit juice and pulp, oil, parsley, ruthmol and pepper; then shake. A clean jam jar is ideal.

Pour over the prepared salad and serve.

Delicious and interesting!

48. *Rosemary's Roast Lamb*

Serves 4-6

Ingredients:
1 leg of lamb
3 cloves of garlic – crushed
  with 1 teaspoon of ruthmol

6 sprigs of fresh rosemary
foil

Garnish: 3 tomatoes, 4 oz (110 g) sweetcorn *or* 4 oz (110 g) peas

Method
1.   Take the joint and cut down the middle to the bone using a very sharp knife. Make two more cuts but this time not quite to the bone and either side of the first cut.

2.   Into the middle cut place a third of the garlic mixture and 2 sprigs of rosemary.

3.   Repeat in the other cuts.

4.   Reshape the joint and tie with string if necessary.

5.   Roast as you would normally do using the foil.

To serve: Cut the tomatoes in half and scoop out the middle. Fill with either the corn or peas. Place the meat on a serving plate and the tomato cups around the joint.

A most impressive dish to serve for Sunday lunch.

49. *Quick Tuna Supper*

Serves 3-4

Ingredients:
8-10 oz (225-275 g) wholemeal
  pasta shells
1 can tuna fish - drained
4-6 oz (110-175 g) mushrooms - washed
  and chopped
1 oz (25 g) vegetable margarine

1 oz (25 g) wholemeal flour
seasoning - black pepper and
  a pinch of ruthmol
10-12 fl oz (275-330 ml) milk
  - cow's, goat's or soya

Method
1.   Cook the pasta shells in water until tender. Drain and put to one side.

2.   Make a mushroom sauce by melting the vegetable margarine and frying the mushrooms until soft but not brown. Remove from the heat and add the flour to make a *roux* - add the milk a little at a time stirring all the time to remove any lumps. Season. Return to the heat stirring continuously and bring slowly to the boil until you have a shiny pouring sauce.

3.   Combine the tuna, sauce and pasta shells and mix well. Turn into a serving dish.

Serve straight away, with triangles of toasted wholemeal bread.

50. *Home-made beefburgers*

You may say, "Why make a beefburger?" A Home Economist can give a dozen good reasons why, but so as not to bore the pants off you I will give only two:
1.   You know what goes into them!

2.   You are getting value for money as your beefburgers will contain only beef, onion, a little cornflour and a few selected spices - no fillers, additives, colourings, flavourings, etc.

Serves 4

Ingredients:
The following will make four ¼ pounders (110 g)
1 lb (450 g) minced beef
1 small onion grated

2 tablesp. cornflour
a pinch of mixed herbs
(parsley and thyme)

Method
1. Put the beef into a bowl, add the onion and herbs and mix well using a wooden spoon.

2. Add one tablespoon of the cornflour and mix until the cornflour is evenly distributed.

3. Divide into four and shape into beefburgers.

4. Coat in the remaining cornflour, then grill or barbecue and serve with your favourite accompaniments.

51. *Wholemeal Pork Pie*

Serves 6-8 portions

Ingredients:
Pastry
11 oz (300 g) wheatmeal flour
1 oz (25 g) cornflour

4½ oz (125 g) vegetable lard
6 tablesp. cold water
1 egg, beaten, size 4

Filling
1¼-1½ lb (560-700 g) 100%
   pork sausagemeat
pinch of herbs – rosemary and
   sage, and a pinch each of
   ruthmol and pepper

2 hard boiled eggs, size 4
1 or 2 eggs beaten, for the glaze

Method
1. *To prepare the pastry*:
(a) Mix the wheatmeal flour and cornflour together thoroughly. Place in a mixing bowl.

58

(b) Heat the water and lard until *just* boiling.

(c) Make a well in the centre of the flour.

(d) Add the beaten egg, then the boiled water and fat and mix thoroughly using a wooden spoon.

(e) When cool knead gently to make smooth.

2.   *To line the tin*: Use a round 7" (18 cm) tin

(a) First line the tin with a piece of foil – there is no need to be too particular – this is just to ensure that the pastry does not stick to the tin.

(b) Take two thirds of the pastry (the remaining third should be kept warm so that a crust does not form on the outside) and

(c) Mould the pastry to the tin ensuring that the pastry is of even thickness.

3.   Place one third of the sausage meat at the bottom of the tin, then add the two hard boiled eggs. Carefully place the remaining sausage meat around the eggs and sprinkle the herbs and seasoning over the sausage meat.

4.   *To put on the lid*:
     Take the remaining one third of the pastry and roll out to $\frac{1}{4}$" (5 mm) thickness. Then wet the pie edge and place the lid on top. Press down, trim and pinch the edges neatly. Make leaves from the remaining pastry and stick to the lid using the egg glaze.

5.   Brush the top with egg glaze and bake at Gas Mark 5, 190°C, 375°F for 50–60 minutes. Glaze every 20 minutes.

6.   After 60 minutes remove the pie from the tin, glaze the sides and then bake for a further 20-25 minutes until you have a deep golden glaze.

7.   Allow to cool, then slice.

Serve with pickles and salad or use as part of a picnic treat.

Sweets

52. Scones

Basic Mixture
8 oz (225 g) wholemeal flour
2 teasp. baking powder
1 oz (25 g) butter, vegetable fat,
  Vitaquell or vegetable margarine :
1 oz (25 g) raw cane sugar
¼ pt (150 ml) goat's milk, cow's milk,
  soya milk or coconut milk*

*If too concentrated dilute to taste

Variations
1. Cheese – Add 2 oz (50 g)
   grated vegetarian cheese (cheddar)
2. Marmite – Add 2 level teasp.
   of Marmite

Method
1.   Place flour in a bowl and stir in the baking powder, mixing thoroughly.

2.   Rub in the fat.

3.   Stir in the sugar.
N.B. If making a savoury variety omit the sugar.

4.   At this point add all the other ingredients if preparing one of the variations.

5.   Add the liquid all at once and mix to a soft dough. Place on a floured surface and gently knead until smooth. Roll out to ¾" (2 cm) thickness and cut out using 2½" (6 cm) cutters. Place onto a greased baking sheet.

6.   Place on the top shelf of a pre-heated oven Gas Mark 7, 220°C, 425°F for 12-15 minutes until well risen and golden brown.

Split and spread with any filling of your choice e.g. peanut butter

53. *Wholemeal Chocolate Cake*

If you are allergic to chocolate, simply replace the cocoa powder with carob powder which is readily available at most health food shops.

Ingredients:

4 oz (110 g) butter, kosher margarine
  * or vegetable fat
  (Vitaquell does not usually make good cakes so I would not personally recommend it.)
4 oz (110 g) raw cane caster sugar
3 eggs, size 4

5-6 oz (150-175 g) wholemeal flour.
plus 2 teaspoons of baking powder
1 oz (25 g) cocoa or ½ oz (10 g) carob powder
2 tablesp. honey

Method

1. Cream fat and sugar together until light and fluffy.

2. Beat eggs in a separate bowl and add to the creamed mixture gradually.

3. Add the honey and beat for one minute.

4. Mix the flour thoroughly with the baking powder and add the cocoa or carob powder.

5. Fold the flour in with a metal spoon. Mix thoroughly.

6. Divide between two greased and lined (only on the bottom) 7″ (18 cm) sandwich tins.

7. Bake for 20-25 minutes until well risen at Gas Mark 4, 180°C, 350°F.

Allow to cool.

Filling:

3 oz vegetable margarine
4 ozs home made icing sugar

Beat together until light and fluffy.

Spread filling on the base and sandwich together.

N.B. This cake freezes well. It is better eaten on the second day as it has time to become more moist.

* See Glossary of Products, p. 146

54. *Apple and Honey Pudding*

Serves 4

Ingredients:
1 tablesp. honey
5 oz (150 g) wholemeal flour,
2 teasps. of cornflour and
2 teasps. of baking powder
2 oz (50 g) butter, kosher margarine*
   or vegetable fat
1 oz (25 g) sultanas

10-12 oz (275-350 g) cooking
   apples, peeled, stewed and
   placed in a 2 pt oven proof
   dish
pinch of cinnamon
2 eggs, size 4, plus
1 tablesp. of water

Method
1.   Place the apple in a dish and put to one side.

2.   Mix the flour, baking powder and cornflour together thoroughly. (Run your fingers through to remove any lumps.)

3.   Rub in the fat and add the sultanas, and cinnamon.

4.   Beat the eggs thoroughly using a fork in a separate bowl and add 1 tablespoon of water.

5.   Add the honey to the dry ingredients. (Do not stir).

6.   Add the liquid all at once to the dry mixture and mix through thoroughly with a spoon for 1-2 minutes.

7.   Place on top of the apple. Put in the oven on the middle shelf for 30-40 minutes until well risen at Gas Mark 4, 180°C, 350°F.
Serve warm or cold.

*See Glossary of products, p. 146

55. *Parsnip Loaf*

Ingredients:
4 oz (110 g) vegetable margarine
5 oz (150 g) raw cane sugar
2 eggs – beaten
8 oz (225 g) wholemeal flour
3 teasp. baking powder

1 teasp. cinnamon
¼ teasp. cloves
1 tablesp. lemon juice
8 oz (225 g) grated parsnips
½ teasp. ruthmol

Method

1. Beat the margarine and sugar until pale in colour.

2. Gradually beat in the eggs.

3. Thoroughly sieve the flour, baking powder, ruthmol and all the other spices; although the bran in the wholemeal flour will separate out it can be easily stirred back in. Add to the mixture folding in.

4. Make the lemon juice up to $\frac{1}{4}$ pt (150 ml) with water, add to the mixture alternatively with the grated parsnip and flour.

5. Grease and line a 2 lb (900 g) loaf tin, add the mixture, and bake at Gas Mark 4, 180°C, 350°F, for 1 hour.

6. Best eaten the next day.

56. *Banana Tea Bread*

Ingredients:

4 oz (110 g) raw cane granulated sugar

3 oz (75 g) vegetable fat or butter

2 eggs, size 4

2 small bananas – peeled and mashed

8 oz (225 g) wholemeal flour and 2 level teaspoons of baking powder

Method

1. Cream fat and sugar together until light and fluffy. Add the egg and beat well.

2. Beat in the bananas.

3. Mix the flour and baking powder well together.

4. Using a metal spoon fold in the flour. Mix thoroughly.

5. Turn into a greased and lined loaf tin.

6. Bake for 40-45 minutes until golden brown at Gas Mark 4-5, 180°C, 350°F.

N.B. Better eaten the next day as the banana flavour develops.

Can be sliced and buttered

57. *Gingerbread*

Ingredients:
12 oz (350 g) wholemeal flour
2 level teasp. ground ginger
2 level teasp. cinnamon
2 level teasp. bicarbonate of soda
8 oz (225 g) vegetable fat, kosher
   margarine or butter

8 oz (225 g) molasses
½ pt (275 ml) milk (goat's, cow's or
   soya)
2 eggs, size 2 – beaten
8 oz (225 g) raw cane sugar

To decorate:
8 oz (225 g) home made icing sugar   4 glaće cherries

Method
1.   Line a roasting tin measuring 13″ x 10″ (32 cm x 25 cm).

2.   Mix the flour, spices and bicarbonate of soda thoroughly and place in a mixing bowl.

3.   Melt the sugar, fat and molasses, but do not allow to boil.

4.   Pour the melted mixture into the mixing bowl, add the milk and beaten egg. Mix well, using a metal spoon.

5.   Pour into the prepared tin and bake for 55-60 minutes at Gas Mark 3, 170°C, 325°F.

6. Allow to cool in the tin and then remove to decorate.

7. Make up the icing sugar into thick spreadable icing with a little water. Spread evenly over the surface and dot the cherries on the top.

Eat the next day.

To give a slightly different taste use 12 ozs (350 g) barley flour instead of the wheat-wholemeal flour.

---

58. *Afternoon Slices*

Ingredients:
4 oz (110 g) butter or vegetable
margarine
4 oz (110 g) chopped dates
3 tablesp. clear honey
5 oz (150 g) wholemeal flour
4 oz (110 g) desiccated coconut

Topping:
8-10 oz (225-275 g) home-made
icing sugar
made up with sufficient lemon
juice to make a runny icing*

Method
1. Melt the fat and honey in a medium sized saucepan.

2. Place all the dry ingredients in a mixing bowl, and pour on the melted mixture. Stir well.

3. Spread onto a greased baking tin measuring 7" x 7" (18 cm x 18 cm).

4. Bake for 20-25 minutes until firm but not crisp at Gas Mark 3, 170°C, 325°F.

5. Remove from the oven and coat with the topping whilst still hot, allowing it to flow to the edges. Allow to cool.

6. Cut into squares and store in a covered tin.

Excellent for packed meals.

* *See A Question of Sugar*, p. 4

59. *Mixed Fruit Crumble*

Serves 4

Ingredients:

Fruit
Combine a selection of soft fruits to a total weight of 1-1½ lbs. My family enjoys the following combination.

1 large Bramley apple	¼ lb (110 g) gooseberries
– peeled and diced	¼ lb (110 g) blackberries
½ lb (225 g) rhubarb	

Simmer together until tender. Sweeten with honey or sugar, according to taste.

Crumble

2 oz (50 g) wholemeal flour and	1 oz (25 g) raw cane sugar
2 teasp. cornflour or rice flour	2 oz (50 g) rye flakes
Mix flours	
2 oz (50 g) vegetable fat or butter	

Rub fat into the flour. Stir in sugar and rye flakes

Method

1.   Place fruit in a 2 pt oven proof dish. Allow to cool slightly.

2.   Sprinkle topping over fruit.

3.   Bake in the centre of the oven for 20-25 minutes until golden brown at Gas Mark 4, 180°C, 350°F.

Serve with yoghurt.

60. *Victoria Sandwich Cake*

A very simple recipe that can be used in many different ways. Once you have mastered the technique you can develop your own ideas of using the basic cake mixture.

Ingredients:
4 oz (110 g) vegetable margarine
  or butter
4 oz (110 g) raw cane caster sugar
2 eggs, size 2

5 oz (125 g) wholemeal flour
½ oz (10 g) cornflour or rice flour
  and 2 teaspoons of baking powder

Method

1. Cream the fat and sugar together until light and fluffy.

2. Beat the eggs in a separate bowl and add gradually to the creamed mixture, beating between each addition.

3. Thoroughly mix together the flour and cornflour mixture making sure the raising agent is evenly distributed.

4. Change to a metal spoon and fold in the flour mixture a little at a time, mixing thoroughly.

5. Divide between two 6″ (15 cm) greased and lined sandwich tins.

6. Bake at Gas Mark 4, 180°C, 350°F for 25-30 minutes until well risen.

7. When cool sandwich together using a filling of your own choice.

---

61. *Pineapple and Rye Up-Side Down Pudding*

Serves 4-6

Ingredients:
1 small can pineapple rings
  (unsweetened are much more
  flavoursome)
4 glacé cherries
2 tablesp. clear honey
6 oz (175 g) ground rye flour and

2 teasp. of baking powder
2 oz (50g) vegetable fat or butter
3 oz (75 g) raw cane sugar
1 lemon – rind and juice
2 eggs, size 2

Method

1. Grease a 2 pint oven proof dish, place the pineapple rings in the bottom. Place the cherries in the centre of the pineapples. Pour over the honey.

2. Place the rye flour and baking powder in a mixing bowl and mix together well.

3. Rub in the fat, stir in the sugar and lemon rind.

4. Beat the eggs in a separate bowl.

5. Add to the mixture and stir, then add the lemon juice and mix thoroughly using a metal spoon.

6. Place the mixture over the pineapple and honey, smooth the surface.

7. Bake on the middle shelf of the oven at Gas Mark 5, 190°C, 375°F for 25-35 minutes until well risen and golden brown.

Turn out onto a plate with the pineapple showing. Serve with a hot sauce e.g. yummie chocolate sauce or custard. As the rye flour gives a rather close, dry texture it needs a moist accompaniment to appreciate its nutty flavour.

62. *Traditional Welsh Cakes*

Makes 14-18 cakes

Ingredients:
6 oz (175 g) wholemeal flour
½ teasp. ruthmol
2 teasp. baking powder
2 oz (50 g) vegetable fat
2 oz (50 g) raw cane sugar
2 oz (50 g) currants
¼ teasp. mixed spice
1/8 pt (75 ml) milk (soya, cow's or goat's)
1 egg, size 2

Method
1. Mix the flour, salt and baking powder well, for even distribution.

2. Rub in the fat.

3. Add the currants, sugar and mixed spice.

4. Beat the egg and milk together, and mix to a soft dough.

5. Roll out to ¼″ (5 mm) thickness, and cut using a 2″ (5 cm) cutter.

6. Cook on a griddle or in a heavy frying pan until evenly brown on both sides. Allow 6-7 minutes for each side.

7. May be eaten hot or cold.

Excellent cold, spread with vegetable margarine or butter, with a thin layer of home made strawberry jam.

63. *Chocolate Fingers*

Ingredients:
4 oz (110 g) vegetable fat or butter
3 dessert spoons golden syrup
1 dessert spoon raw cane sugar
2 dessert spoons cocoa or
   1 dessertspoon carob powder
3 dessert spoons golden syrup

2 oz (50 g) dried fruit
4 oz (110 g) cooking chocolate
  – milk or plain
1 packet wholewheat digestive
  biscuits – broken up*

*You must check the packet for any ingredients to which you are allergic. Allinson's are the most reliable.

Method
1. Melt the syrup and fat but do not allow to boil.

2. Add the cocoa or carob powder, fruit, sugar and lastly the crushed biscuits.

3. Mix well and then press into a greased shallow tin. Place in the fridge for ten minutes to cool.

4. Melt the cooking chocolate in a bowl over a pan of hot water and spread over the top of the mixture.

5. Cut into fingers when cold and store in a tin.

64. *Fresh Fruit in Yoghurt*

Serves 4

Ingredients:
2 bananas – peeled
1 ripe mango – peeled
1 small fresh pineapple

3 tablesp. demerara sugar
2 tablesp. honey
1-pint carton thick and creamy
  natural yoghurt

69

Method

1. Peel the pineapple, remove the hard centre core with a core remover, cut into "bite size" pieces, place in a mixing bowl.

2. Peel and chop the bananas and mango and add to the bowl.

3. Stir in the honey.

4. Spoon into a heat-proof dish (2 pint (1.1 litre) size) and pour the yoghurt over.

5. Sprinkle the demerara sugar on top and place under a pre-heated grill for 2-3 minutes until the sugar has melted and gone dark brown in colour.

Serve at once.

Miscellaneous

65. *Candied Peel*

I feel that if you can make it – you should! Why? Because you will use only pure ingredients and not add the colourings and preservatives to be found in many marketed products. That is why I have included candied peel, and I hope once you have tried your own you will never buy any more.

Ingredients:

The sound, fresh peel of lemons, oranges or grapefruit

1 lb (450 g) raw cane sugar to every 6 skins
salt

Candy at least 6 skins at one time

Method

1.   Cut the peel into convenient sized pieces.

2.   Soak for 48 hours in salted water.

3.   Drain and put the peel into a pan with water and simmer until tender.

4.   Drain and place in a basin.

5.   Using 1 lb (450 g) sugar to ½ pint (275 ml) of water boil syrup for 10 minutes.

6.   Pour the syrup over the peel, cover and stand for 7 days.

7.   Pour off the syrup and re-boil, add the peel and boil until the peel is clean and the syrup evaporates.

8.   Place on a greased try and sprinkle with sugar and leave in a warm place to dry and candy.

Store in an air tight tin.

---

66. *Christmas Cake*

Ingredients:

14 oz (400 g) sultanas*
9 oz (250 g) raisins*
9 oz (250 g) currants*
4 oz (110 g) stoned and chopped prunes*
4 oz (110 g) mixed peel
4 fl oz (110 ml) sherry, cider
   or grape juice
4 oz (110 g) glacé cherries
1 orange – rind and juice‡
1 lemon – rind and juice‡

10 oz (275 g) kosher margarine,
   butter or vegetable margarine
10 oz (275 g) muscovado sugar
14 oz (400 g) wholemeal flour and
½ teap. baking powder
1 teasp. ground cinnamon
1 teasp. mixed spice
6 free range eggs, size 2
2 tablesp. apricot jam
1½ tablesp. molasses

* Please remember to buy fruit that has not been coated in Mineral oil.
‡ Wash before use.

Method

1.   Wash and dry the dried fruit. Put into a large saucepan with the prunes, add the juice from the lemon and orange.

2.   Add the cider, grape juice or sherry and heat until steaming, stirring all the time. Cook for 3-4 minutes.

3.   Place in a bowl with any remaining juice, cover and leave for 12 hours.

4.   Add the peel and cherries to the fruit mixture.

5.   In a large mixing bowl cream the fat and sugar together until fluffy.

6.   Beat the eggs in a separate bowl.

7.   Sieve the dry ingredients together.

8.   Add the egg and flour mixture alternatively until all is well mixed.

9.   Mix in the jam and molasses.

10.   Mix in the fruits – I find using a spatula is more effective although a wooden spoon is adequate.

11.   Place the mixture in a double lined cake tin: Round 9″ (23 cm) or Square 10″ (25 cm)

Smooth the top and make a small dip in the centre. Bake at Gas Mark 1, 140°C, 275°F for 4½ hours.
Test with a skewer – it should come out clean – allow a further 15 minutes if necessary.

Remove the cake and keep in a tin until you intend to almond paste.

Some people place a cut apple in the tin to encourage the cake to become more moist.

67. *Home-made Mincemeat*

Because manufacturers use suet in their mincemeat it is unsuitable for someone allergic to white flour – because the suet has been tossed in the flour to keep the pieces separate.

After you have tried this excellent recipe you will always make your own as it is so simple and quick.

Ingredients:

4 lb (1 kg 800 g) Bramley apples
  – peeled and chopped
8 oz (225 g) candied peel – home-
  made (see recipe on p. 71)
10 oz (275 g) butter, vegetable
  margarine or kosher margarine
1 lb (450 g) raw cane sugar

1 lb (450 g) raisins – washed
¾ lb (350 g) sultanas – washed
½ lb (225 g) currants – washed
1 teasp. mixed spice
1 teasp. cinnamon
½ teasp. nutmeg

Use a large preserving pan or two large saucepans, making two batches.

Method

1. Place the apples in a preserving pan together with the fat and sugar. Simmer until the apple has pulped.

2. Add the washed fruits and candied peel and stir in well.

3. Add the spcies and mix thoroughly.

4. Return to the heat and simmer gently until most of the liquid has disappeared.

5. Allow to cool and then place in clean, dry jam jars or place in the freezer in plastic containers.

73

68. *Wholemeal Salad Cream*

Makes 3-4 jars

Ingredients:
6 oz (175 g) raw cane sugar
   - granulated
3 oz (75 g) wholemeal flour
4 teasp. dry mustard powder*

1 pt (570 ml) milk (cow's, goat's
   or soya)
1 egg, size 2
1 pt (570 ml) vinegar

Method

1.   Mix all the dry ingredients together in a large saucepan.

2.   Add the beaten egg, and then the milk.

3.   Lastly, add the vinegar.

4.   Bring slowly to the boil stirring contantly until the mixture is thick and smooth.

5.   Pour into clean and sterilised jars. Cover with wax paper and seal.

N.B. If the cream is too thick for use thin with vinegar until it reaches the desired consistency.

*French mustard may be used to give variety in flavour. Ensure that it does not contain white flour before you use it.

69. *Apricot and Sultana Cake*

Ingredients:

6 oz (175 g) vegetable margarine
   or butter
6 oz (175 g) raw cane sugar
3 eggs, size 2
6 oz (175 g) wholemeal flour, and
3 teaspoons cornflour and
2 teaspoons of baking powder

8 oz (225 g) dried apricots
8 oz (225 g) sultanas
rind and juice of ½ lemon
½ pt (275 ml) water

Method

1.   Simmer the apricots with ½ pt (275 ml) water until tender and the liquid has disappeared. Allow to cool, then chop.

2.   Beat the fat and sugar together until light and fluffy.

3.   Beat the eggs in a separate bowl and gradually add to the mixture. Beat well between additions.
   If the mixture should curdle add a little flour which will correct this minor problem.

4.   Beat in the apricots and the rind and juice of the lemon.

5.   Mix the sultanas with the flour mixture.

6.   Using a metal spoon fold in the remaining dry ingredients. Ensure all is well mixed.

7.   Turn into a greased and lined baking tin measuring round 6"-7" (15 cm-18 cm). Bake low down in the oven at Gas Mark 4, 180°C, 350°F for 1¾ hours. Lower the temperature towards the end of the cooking time if the cake becomes rather brown.

N.B. Leave in the tin to cool.

Store covered in foil. Better eaten the next day.

70. *Bread Sauce*

Ingredients:
½ pt (275 ml) milk (Soya is best,
  but you can use goat's or
  even cow's)
pinch of ruthmol
1 small onion

½ teasp. ground cloves
½ teasp. black pepper
4–6 oz (110–175 g) wholemeal
  bread crumbs
knob of vegetable fat or butter

Method
1.   Simmer the onion in the liquid to extract the flavour, and then discard the onion.

2.   Add the ground cloves, ruthmol and black pepper.

3.   Sprinkle on the breadcrumbs and mix well. Check the seasoning and adjust if necessary.

4.   Place in a warm serving dish and put the knob of butter on top. Excellent to accompany chicken and turkey.

CORN-FREE RECIPES

How innocent a humble cob of corn looks growing tall and becoming ripe and golden at maturity, but for those who have an intolerance to corn it will mean constant vigilance, for corn is to be found not only as sweet corn kernels, but is also given to poultry as their main food sources. So if you show allergic reactions to corn you may well be advised to stay clear of poultry and eggs too. This limits your possible foods but nevertheless should not prevent you from having an interesting and varied diet.

Here is a list of other items in everyday use which also contain corn:

1. Adhesives on envelopes and postage stamps.

2. Most tablets for medication e.g. aspirin – corn is often used to fill out the tablets and so make them a suitable size.

3. Bourbon and others whiskies.

4. Capsules, lozenges, suppositories and vitamin tablets.

5. Monosodium glutamate – sometimes called "Chinese taste powder".

6. Chewing gum.

7. Talcum powder.

8. Soya bean milk – not all varieties, so check packet contents.

9. Chinese cooking – the Chinese use corn a great deal as a thickening agent.

10 Soups commercially prepared – the cream and thickened varieties.

11. Cough syrups and many other syrupy liquid medicinal preparations.

12. Almost all baking mixes for pancakes, doughnuts, pastry, cakes and batters.

13. Pie fillings.

14. Some preserves.

15. Commercially prepared salad dressings.

16. Gravy and sauce mixes which are usually termed "instant variety".

17. Cornflakes and some other breakfast cereals.

18. Sandwich spreads.

19. Popcorn.

20. Starch – sometimes it is just an ingredient listed on a less obvious item.

21. Chocolates and other sweet confectionery.

22. Beers.

23. Biscuits – corn helps to make the texture of the finished product more crumbly so it is usually added to most varieties. Keep checking the ingredients list.

It seems from my own investigations that Americans show a more frequent allergic response to corn than people in other countries. Nevertheless, it is still one of the foods that I feel needs bringing to people's attention. There is also a necessity to show how one can eliminate an everyday foodstuff without suffering nutritionally.

The recipes in the following chapter have been carefully devised to be nutritionally sound, interesting and relatively simple to prepare.

Corn-free – A week's planned menu

	Breakfast	*Lunch*	*Tea/Supper*
Monday	Cleansing breakfast: juice of lemon in a glass of warm water 1 bowl of muesli fresh juice - orange or grape	Roll Mop Herrings Salad Printanière	½ avocado with lemon juice 6 ozs grilled steak watercress and orange salad
Tuesday	half a grapefruit with honey	Cold Corned Beef Risotto Beansprout Salad	Sorrel Soup with wholemeal toasted bread
Wednesday	Florida Cocktail	Salad Platter wholemeal bread and butter Fresh fruit	Tuna Pie fresh vegetables Wholemeal fruit Flan
Thursday	Cold stewed prunes	Mackerel Pâté toasted wholemeal bread slice of water melon	Pork Goulash Brown rice Summer fruit kebabs
Friday	Beans on wholemeal toast	Cottage Layer Pie Crunchie Date Dessert	Dutch Mussel Supper Crusty wholemeal bread oriental fruit salad
Saturday	Porridge with sultanas and honey	8 oz (225 g) grilled meat e.g. steak, pork chops Printanière - simple salad fresh fruit	Pork and bean casserole a selection of boiled vegetables fresh fruit
Sunday	Tropical Muesli	Peppered Beef a selection of fresh vegetables and boiled potatoes French Apple Flan	Fruity Jack toasted cheese sandwiches Raspberry Ice Cream

CORN-FREE RECIPES

Starters

71. *Mushroom Soup*

Serves 4

Ingredients:
8-10 oz (225-275 g) fresh
  mushrooms
1 pt (570 ml) stock - meat or
  vegetable water
1 pt (570 ml) milk (cow's,
  goat's or soya)

3 tablesp. wholemeal flour
2 oz (50 g) vegetable fat
  or butter
2 teasp. salt or ruthmol,
6 black peppercorns

Method
1. Stew the mushrooms for 5 minutes in the stock. Add the salt or ruthmol and 6 black peppercorns.

2. Liquidise or chop the mushrooms.

3. Make a roux* sauce by melting the fat, adding the flour and blending in the milk and bringing to the boil for 3 minutes stirring all the time until thick and smooth.

4. Add the mushroom mixture and stir, adjust the seasoning if necessary.

Serve straight away, otherwise a skin will form and may cause lumps in the soup if stirred in.

* See Boeuf aux champignons, p. 49 for Roux method.

72. *Broad Bean Spread*

Ingredients:
6 oz (175 g) dried broad beans
1 oz (25 g) dried lentils
3 tablesp. olive oil
2½ teasp. lemon juice

½ teasp. salt
1 tablesp. chopped parsley
8 stoned black olives

Method

1. Wash the beans and lentils in a sieve under a running tap until clean.

2. Place in a pressure cooker with ½ pint (275 ml) of water and allow to cook for 45 minutes using 15 lb pressure.
The beans should be tender – if not, cook for a further 5-10 minutes. Allow to cool and retain the liquid.

3. In a liquidiser add the oil, lemon juice and salt and liquidise for 2 minutes.

4. Add the beans and sufficient liquid to make a smooth spread.

5. Turn into individual dishes and sprinkle with the chopped parsley and garnish with the olives.

Serve at room temperature with rye bread.

---

73. *Mackerel Pâté*

Serves 4

Ingredients:

10 oz (275 g) smoked mackerel
  – boned and skinned
4 oz (110 g) fat – kosher margarine,
  butter or Vitaquell

4 oz (110 g) cottage cheese – sieved
1 lemon – ½ for the juice and
  ½ for the decoration
parsley for decoration

Method

1. Place the mackerel in a bowl and mash thoroughly with a fork.

2. Melt the fat and add to the fish along with the lemon juice and cream cheese.

3. Beat well and place in a ¾ pt (425 ml) serving dish.

4. Place in the fridge to set.

5. Decorate with lemon wedges and parsley.

Serve with thin slices of rye bread or wholemeal bread.

74. *Florida Cocktail*

Serves 4

Ingredients:
3 grapefruits
3 oranges – sweet and juicy
2 tablesp. sherry
2 glaće cherries – halved

4 sprigs of mint, washed and dipped into caster sugar – set aside
4 glass serving dishes

Method

1. Peel the fruits using the Savoy method – cut off the top of the oranges and grapefruits then peel them using a very sharp knife. Cut through the peel and pith but do not remove the flesh. It is easier if you have your knife at a 45° angle. If you are really adept you will be able to take the peel off in one strip.

2. Take the peeled fruits and cut into segments using the same sharp knife. Place in a mixing bowl – ensure that none of the white pith escapes your knife. Squeeze out any remaining juice from the skin and then discard.

3. Add the sherry and stir well. Leave for 2 hours in the fridge to allow the flavours to develop.

4. *To serve*: place in chilled glass dishes and top with the sugared mint and cherries.

Excellent to start any meal, or as a dessert, or for breakfast.

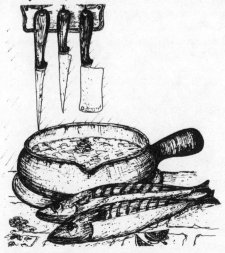

75. *Terrine of Pork*

Serves 4-6

Ingredients:

1 lb (450 g) sausage meat
  – 100% meat variety containing
  no rusk
1 lb (450 g) minced pork
  – any cut will do (Your
  butcher may be kind enough
  to mince it for you.)

3 slices boiled ham
a good pinch of black pepper
½ teasp. ruthmol
2 cloves garlic – crushed

Method

1.   Take a terrine which is an oven proof glazed casserole dish often square in shape, 2-2½ pint (1.1-1.4 litre) size with a lid.

2.   Season the sausage meat with the black pepper and ruthmol and the crushed garlic and do the same with the minced pork.

3.   To prepare the pâté place half of the sausage meat in the terrine, top with one slice of the ham then place half the minced pork on top followed by the other slice of the ham then place the remaining minced pork on top followed by the other slice of ham. Top with the remaining sausage meat.

4.   Cover with the lid or foil and put into a bain marie, which is a baking tray half filled with water.

5.   Place in a moderate oven Gas Mark 3-4, 170°C, 325°F. Cook for two hours. Allow to cool and store in the fridge. Use within 7 days of making.

Main Courses

76. Roll Mop Herrings

Serves 4

Ingredients:
4 fresh and cleaned herrings
1 blade of mace
10 peppercorns

¼ teasp. ruthmol
1/8 pt (75 ml) water
¼ pt (150 ml) cider vinegar

Method
1.   Wash and clean the fish. If you cannot deal with the fish yourself ask the fishmonger to bone it for you.

2.   Roll up the fish beginning at the tail end.

3.   Pack the fish into an oven proof dish – large enough so that the lid does not touch the fish.

4.   Sprinkle the spices over the fish. Pour over the vinegar and water.

5.   Place in a casserole dish with a lid. If you haven't a casserole dish with a lid, an ovenproof dish covered with foil may be used.

6.   Bake in the centre of the oven for 45 minutes at Gas Mark 2, 150°C, 300°F.

7.   Allow to cool with the lid on.

Serve cold with a salad.

77. Cold Corned Beef Risotto

Serves 4

Ingredients:
8 oz (225 g) brown rice
2 tablesp. soya oil
2 tablesp. tomato purée
½ pt (275 ml) stock or water
1 bay leaf
ruthmol and black pepper

1 small red pepper – diced
4 oz (110 g) cooked butter beans
1 onion peeled and chopped
12 oz (350 g) can corned beef –
   diced
parsley to garnish

Method

1.   Heat the oil and add the rice and onion and cook for 2-3 minutes.

2.   Add the liquid, tomato purée, bay leaf, ruthmol and black pepper. Simmer for 10-15 minutes.

3.   Add the diced pepper and continue cooking until the rice is tender. You may have to add more liquid if the rice is not cooked.

4.   When cooked allow to cool and then stir in the butter beans and diced corned beef.

5.   Turn onto a plate and sprinkle with the parsley.

Serve with wedges of tomato.

---

78. *Pork Goulash*

Serves 4

Ingredients:
1-1¼ lb (450-560 g) pork - meat
   from the leg or tenderloin
2 tablesp. soya oil
1 large green pepper -
   trimmed and sliced
lb (225 g) French beans -
   fresh or frozen
½ pint (275 ml) water
1 large heavy bottomed casserole dish 2½-3 pints (1.4-1.7 litres) in size

1 tube tomato purée
1-2 cloves garlic - crushed
a pinch each of black pepper
   and ruthmol
1 teasp. paprika
4 oz carton natural goat's
   milk yoghurt

Method

1.   Cut the meat into cubes.

2.   Heat the oil in the casserole and add the meat, crushed garlic, paprika, black pepper and ruthmol. Cook for 5 minutes.

3.   Stir in the tomato purée.

4.   Add the water and bring to the boil. Place in a moderate oven Gas Mark 3, 170°C, 325°F for 2 hours.

5.   Half an hour before the cooking time is up, add the sliced pepper and french beans. Cook until tender.

6.   *To serve*: Top with the yoghurt but do not reboil otherwise it will curdle.

Serve with boiled brown rice and a selection of fresh vegetables.

79. *Cottage Layer Pie*

Serves 4

Ingredients:
1 lb (450 g) minced beef
1 onion – peeled and
   chopped
½ pt (275 ml) stock or water
2 tablespoons tomato purée
4–6 oz (110–175 g) peas – cooked

8 oz (225 g) sliced carrots
   – cooked
1½ lb (700 g) potatoes – peeled,
   boiled and mashed with
   a little milk

Method
1.   Brown the mince in a saucepan, add the onion and cook for 7-10 minutes.

2.   Add the ½ pt (275 ml) liquid and simmer for 30-40 minutes or until the majority of the liquid has evaporated. Stir in the tomato purée.

3.   Place the meat in a 2½ pt (1.4 litre) ovenproof dish.

4.   Arrange the carrots on top, then the peas.

5.   Using a forcing bag and nozzle pipe the mashed potato on top.

6.   Bake for a further 20 minutes until the potato is crisp and golden brown at Gas Mark 4-5, 180°C, 350°F.

A quick and economical mid-week supper dish.

---

80. *Tuna Pie*

Serves

Ingredients:

1 medium onion	2 sticks of celery
12 oz (350 g) potato – grated	2 oz (50 g) wholemeal bread
salt and pepper	crumbs
1 egg	2 oz (50 g) vegetarian cheese
fresh parsley	if allowed
2 oz (50 g) butter or vegetable margarine	1 small can tuna fish – flaked

Method

1.   Grate half the onion. Mix with the potato and add the seasoning.

2.   Grease the flan dish and then press the mixture into the flan dish, making sure the sides are level.

3.   Melt 1½ oz (40 g) of the fat and pour over the potato base.

4.   Melt the remaining butter and grate the remaining onion, chop the celery, and gently fry together until soft.

5.   Stir in the flaked tuna, bread crumbs and beaten egg. Add the parsley. Spoon into the base.

6.   Cover with foil and bake at Gas Mark 4, 180°C, 350°F, for 30-35 minutes. Ten minutes from the end remove the foil, sprinkle grated cheese on top and allow to become golden brown.

Decorate with slices of tomato and garnish with parsley.

Although this recipe contains egg, you can omit it if you wish.

81. *Peppered Beef*

Serves 4

Ingredients:
1¼-1½ lb (560-675 g) stewing steak
2 green peppers –
    trimmed and diced
½ teasp. ruthmol
1 teasp. ground ginger

2 tablesp. soya oil
pinch of black pepper
1 large can of pineapple
    cubes
2 tablesp. soya sauce

Method
1.   Trim the meat and cut into cubes.

2.   Heat the oil in a heavy casserole dish and brown the meat, stirring all the time.

3.   Add the ginger, black pepper, pineapple cubes and juice, and ruthmol. Top up with a little water to cover the meat.

4.   Cook very slowly for 2 hours in a low oven, Gas Mark 2, 150°C, 300°F.

5.   Half an hour before serving add the prepared green peppers and soya sauce.

Serve with boiled brown rice.

82. *Dutch Mussel Supper*

Serves 4

Ingredients:
1 lb (450 g) cooked mussels
    – cleaned and drained
8 oz (225 g) dutch cheese
    e.g. Gouda
1 lb (450 g) tin of tomatoes

a good pinch of black pepper
a pinch of ruthmol
2-3 oz (50-75 g) melted butter
1 clove of garlic – crushed
3 tablesp. chopped parsley

Method

1. Place the mussels in a casserole dish.

2. Grate the cheese and sprinkle over the mussels.

3. Drain the tomatoes and place on top.

4. Melt the butter in a small saucepan and add the black pepper, ruthmol and crushed garlic and pour over the tomatoes.

5. Finally sprinkle with the parsley.

6. Cook uncovered in a hot oven for 25-30 minutes at Gas Mark 5, 190°C, 375°F.

Serve with slices of wholemeal pitta bread that has been warmed in the oven.

---

83. *Pork and Bean Casserole*

Serves 4

Ingredients:
1 lb (450 g) belly of pork
4-6 oz (110-175 g) dried butter beans
1 large onion – peeled and chopped
2 medium cooking apples
  – peeled and stewed

a good pinch each of black
  pepper and ruthmol
1½ pts (345 ml) of water to cook
  the beans in

Method

1. Soak the beans overnight in the 1½ pints (345 ml) of water. Transfer to a saucepan and boil for 50-60 minutes until tender. Place in a medium sized casserole dish.

2. Cut the pork into 3″ (7.5 cm) strips and place on the beans.

3. Add the chopped onion and a good pinch each of black pepper and ruthmol.

4. Cover with the stewed apple and cook covered for 2 hours at Gas Mark 2/3, 300°F, 150°C.

Serve with a selection of freshly cooked green vegetables e.g. cabbage, broccoli, spinach.

84. *Printanière – Simple Salad*

Serves

Ingredients:

1 medium crisp lettuce	1 bunch of watercress
– Webbs is ideal	3 tablesp. chives – diced

1 bunch of dandelion leaves (taken from the fields and not too close to the roads otherwise they may have exhaust particles on them which may contain lead). Take young tender leaves only from the middle of the plant.

Method

1.   Wash and dry the leaves. Discard any damaged leaves.

2.   Shred the lettuce, watercress and dandelion leaves. Place in a salad bowl and toss.

3.   *Dressing*:   4 tablespoons olive or soya oil
2 tablespoons wine or cider vinegar
pinch of basil, black pepper, tarragon,
rosemary, clove of garlic – crushed.

Combine together and shake in a clean jar. A jam jar is ideal.

4.   Pour the dressing over the prepared leaves and toss well with salad servers.

Complete by sprinkling with the prepared chives.

Serve straight away.

85. *Fish Kebabs*

Serves 4

Ingredients:
1-1½ lb (450-675 g) fresh cod –
   the thick parts give
   better results
1 large green pepper
1 large red pepper
32 large green grapes
   (smaller quantities may be used)

tomato wedges
2 lemons
a good pinch each of black
   pepper and ruthmol
8 skewers

Method
1.   Trim the fish and cut into even sized pieces.

2.   Trim the peppers and cut into cubes.

3.   Thread the ingredients onto the skewers ensuring that each kebab contains an equal quantity of food.

4.   Using one of the lemons squeeze the juice over the kebabs and sprinkle with the pepper and ruthmol. Leave for one hour in the fridge for the flavours to develop.

5.   Cook 15-20 minutes on a barbecue.

6.   Serve on a bed of lettuce with a wedge of lemon to squeeze over.

To make the meal a little more filling and nutritious serve with triangles of buttered wholemeal bread.

86. *Aubergine and Ham Supper*

Serves 4

Ingredients:
1 large aubergine
4-6 oz (110-175 g) cooked ham
  – cut into strips

1 large can of tomatoes
pinch of dill seed
4-6 oz (110-175 g) wholemeal
   bread crumbs

Method

1. Wash the aubergine and prick with a fork. Place on a baking sheet and place in a moderate oven at Gas Mark 4-5, 180°C, 350°F, for 30-35 minutes until soft.

2. Allow to cool slightly then mash with a fork. If the skin is tough, chop with a sharp knife.

3. Place in a 2 pint (1.1 litre) ovenproof dish.

4. Sprinkle with the strips of ham.

5. Pour over the tin of tomatoes and mash slightly.

6. Sprinkle the dill seed over and top with the bread crumbs.

7. Bake uncovered for 30 minutes until thoroughly heated and golden brown at Gas Mark 4, 180°C, 350°F.

---

87. *Tandoori Lamb Cutlets*

Serves 3-4

Ingredients:
4-6 lamb cutlets

Tandoori sauce:
10 fl oz (275 ml) goat's milk natural yoghurt
1 teaspoon chili powder
½ teaspoon ground ginger

2 cloves of garlic – crushed
1 tablespoon cider vinegar
1 onion – chopped

Method

1. Liquidise all the tandoori sauce ingredients for 2-3 minutes.

2. Put the lamb cutlets into a bowl and pour over the sauce, leave for 2 hours for the flavours to mingle.

3. Place all the ingredients into a baking tray and bake uncovered for 30-40 minutes until the meat is cooked at Gas Mark 5, 190°C, 375°F. Baste with the sauce throughout the cooking time.

4. Serve with boiled long grain brown rice with the sauce poured over the meat.

A little extra yoghurt may be added if necessary to give sufficient sauce to moisten the meat.

A simple green salad may also be served.

88. *Pork – Elizabethan Style*

Serves 4

Ingredients:

1 lb (450 g) pork – meat from the leg or tenderloin
2 large onions – sliced
1 large cooking apple – peeled and sliced
2 sticks of celery – diced
2-3 oz (50-75 g) prunes – chopped
2 oz (50 g) almonds

¼ pt (150 ml) fresh orange juice
a good pinch of black pepper
a good pinch of ruthmol
1 grapefruit *or* orange cut into segments
a pinch of mixed herbs – sage, thyme, basil
2 tablespoons of oil

Method

1. Cut the pork into cubes.

2. Heat the oil and toss the meat to seal in the flavour. Add the sliced onions and celery. Cook for 2-3 minutes.

3. Add all the other ingredients and bring slowly to the boil.

4. Place in a moderate oven, Gas Mark 4-5, 180°C, 350°F, for 1-1½ hours until the meat is tender.

Serve with boiled brown rice or jacket potatoes.

N.B. A heavy casserole dish is ideal for cooking this recipe, 2½-3 pint (1.4-1.7 litre) size.

Sweets

89. *Melon and Peach Salad*

Serves 4-6

Ingredients:
2 small cantaloup melons
2 medium sized ripe peaches
4 oz (110 g) raw cane caster sugar

2½ tablesp. fresh lemon juice
2 teasp rose water (optional)

Method

1. Cut the melons in half. Remove the pips and stringy pulp.

2. Make as many melon balls as possible using a melon ball scoop.

3. Blanch the peaches in a bowl of boiling water and peel off the skins. Cut lengthwise, and then cut into ¼" (5 mm) slices.

4. Add the peaches, sugar, lemon juice and rose water to the melon balls and gently toss.

5. Cover with cling film and leave in the fridge for 2-4 hours for the flavours to mingle.

Spoon the salad into sundae dishes and sprinkle with a little crushed ice.

90. *Wholemeal Sponge Flan*

Serves 4–6

Ingredients:
2 eggs, size 2
2 oz (50 g) icing sugar (raw cane)
2 oz (50 g) wholemeal flour and
1 heaped teaspoon corn flour

Filling:
fresh summer fruits e.g. peaches,
  strawberries, raspberries
tinned fruits e.g. pears, apri-
  apricots, mixed fruits
arrowroot glaze – see below
  for ingredients and method

Method
1.   Prepare the flan by whisking the eggs and sugar until the mixture is thick and creamy or until you can leave a trail of the figure of 8 on the surface for the count of 4.

2.   Mix the two flours together thoroughly and then fold in the flour mixture using a metal spoon, taking care not to miss any of the flour which may settle at the bottom of the bowl.

3.   Prepare the flan tin – I always grease if using a non-stick tin, but grease *and* line an ordinary tin.

4.   Bake for 12 minutes at Gas Mark 7, 220° C, 425° F until well risen.

5.   Allow to cool and fill with fruit.

6.   To make the arrowroot glaze use:
       1 heaped tablespoon arrowroot
       1 dessert spoonful of clear honey
       ⅓ pt (205 ml) water

   (a) Mix all the ingredients together.
   (b) Bring to the boil, slowly stirring all the time until clear and thick.
   (c) Stir until slightly cooled and then pour over all the fruit ensuring all the fruit is coated. This ensures that all the fruit there remains moist.

Eat on the day the flan is made.

If you wish to make the flan in advance it will freeze but should only be frozen for up to two weeks as it may dry out if left too long. Ensure that it is well covered and labelled with the date of making.

91. *Raspberry Ice Cream*

Serves 4

Ingredients:
¼ pt (150 ml) goat's milk
4 oz (110 g) vegetable fat,
  Vitaquell or butter
1 teasp. gelatine
1 lb (450 g) raspberries
  (fresh or frozen)

2 large egg whites
½ lb (225 g) raw cane caster
  sugar
¼ pt (150 ml) water

Stage 1

Method
1. Heat the goat's milk, fat and gelatine until melted and mix together.

2. Pour into a liquidiser and liquidise for 2 minutes. Pour into a bowl and set. Reserve until required.

Stage 2

1. Sieve or liquidise the raspberries and reserve until required.

2. Bring the water and sugar to the boil and then simmer steadily for 5 minutes to allow the syrup to form.

3. In a clean bowl beat the egg whites until stiff. The test for this is to turn the bowl upside down. If the mixture slides keep beating, but if the mixture remains then the mixture is ready for use.

4. Keep beating whilst adding the boiling syrup in a steady stream.

5. Beat until thick and stiff. Leave for 5 minutes and re-beat until cool.

6. Using a large metal spoon fold in the goat's milk mixture along with the liquidised raspberries. Turn into a plastic tub and freeze.

Use within 3 weeks of making.

A domestic fridge frozen foods compartment is not really satisfactory for ice-cream making as the temperature is not really low enough. A freezer is really required to obtain the best results.

92. *Crunchy Date Dessert*

Ingredients:

4 oz (110 g) chopped dates
¼ pt (150 ml) water or coconut
  milk
4 oz (110 g) oats

1½ oz (40 g) wholemeal flour
2 oz (50 g) vegetable margarine
  or butter
1½ oz (40 g) raw cane sugar

Method

1. Simmer dates in the liquid then put to one side and allow to cool.

2. Rub the fat into the flour and oats. Stir in the sugar.

3. Press half of the oat mixture into a 6″ (15 cm) sandwich tin.

4. Pour over the date mixture and spread out evenly on top.

5. Sprinkle the other half of the oat mixture on top.

6. Bake at Gas Mark 4, 180°C, 350°F for 40 minutes.

Cut into portions and serve with a plain sweet sauce flavoured with vanilla.

93. *Summer Fruit Kebabs*

Serves 4

Cut 8 10″ (25 mm) long stems from a mint bush.
Remove the leaves and put to one side.
Wash the stems and leaves.

Ingredients for Kebabs

1 lb (450 g) strawberries – whole
2 kiwi fruits – cut in half,
  then in quarters
½ lb (225 g) ripe apricots – halved
half a honeydew melon – cut
  into squares or balls with a scooper

Glaze:

Boil up ¼ pint (150 ml) of water,
2 dessert spoonfuls of sugar and
1 tablespoon of Cointreau

Method

1. Thread the fruit onto the stems.

2. Brush the glaze onto the fruit.

3. Grill or barbecue.

4. Repeat, brushing with the glaze again.

Serve on a plate decorated with mint leaves and a glass of champagne!

---

94. *Oriental Fruit Salad*

Makes 4 generous portions

Ingredients:

8 oz (225 g) fresh lychees
  (canned will do)
1 small pineapple –
  peeled and cored
2 kiwi fruits

1 large banana
¼-½ pt (150-275 ml) syrup – made
  from ½ pt (275 ml) water
  and 4 oz (110 g) cane sugar

Method

1. Prepare the syrup by boiling the sugar and water together for 3 minutes. Allow to cool and pour into a glass serving bowl.

2. If using fresh lychees peel carefully, cut in half and remove the stone. Place in a glass serving bowl and use the juice obtained in place of the syrup. If using canned lychees place straight into the glass serving bowl, with the ready made syrup.

3. Take the peeled and cored pineapple and cut into bite size pieces and add to the bowl.

4. Peel the kiwi fruit carefully so as not to remove too much of the green flesh. Slice into 1/8″ (3 mm) slices (keep 5 slices for decoration) and add to the bowl.

5. Peel and slice the banana. Add to the fruit salad.

6. Mix carefully and allow to stand for 2 hours in a cool place to allow the flavours to develop.

95. *French Apple Flan* – *using a rich wholemeal pastry*

Serves

Ingredients
for a 10" (25 mm) flan dish:
7 oz (200 g) wholemeal flour
and 1 oz (25 g) rice flour
4 oz (110 g) butter or
   vegetable margarine
1½ oz (40 g) raw cane sugar
1 egg, size 4 and 3 tablesp.
   of cold water, *or*
   6-8 tablesp. cold water

Filling:

2 lb (900g) cooking apples –
   peeled and cored
6-8 oz (175-225 g) apricot jam*
3 tablesp. water

* low sugar jam would be ideal to
   reduce the total sugar content

Method
1. Rub the fat into the flour mixture. Stir in the sugar.

2. Mix to a dough using the water and egg. Knead until smooth. Allow to relax for 10 minutes in the fridge. This will help stop the pastry from shrinking when baked.

3. Line a 10" (25 cm) flan dish, either china or metal.

4. Take the apples and slice them and then arrange the slices in circles in the flan dish.

5. Put the jam and water into a pan and heat gently until melted and thoroughly mixed.

6. Pour the jam mixture over the prepared flan dish and bake for 35-40 minutes at Gas Mark 4, 180°C, 350°F, until golden brown.

Serve hot or cold.

96. *Raspberry Buns*

A simple and easy tea-time treat. Delicious freshly made and eaten hot.

Makes 6-8

Ingredients:
8 oz (225 g) flour – wholemeal
  or white
1½ teasp. baking powder
1 oz (25 g) vegetable fat or butter

1 oz (25 g) raw cane sugar
¼ pt (150 ml) milk (goat's,
  cow's or soya)
4 tablesp. raspberry jam

Method
1. Mix the flour and baking powder together until evenly distributed.

2. Rub in the fat using your finger tips.

3. Stir in the sugar using a metal spoon.

4. Add the liquid all at once and mix to a dough. Knead gently until smooth.

5. Roll into 6-8 even sized balls. Place on a greased baking sheet.

6. Using a floured finger make little holes in the centre of each bun and fill with raspberry jam.

7. Bake in the middle/top of an oven at Gas Mark 6, 200°C, 400°F, for 12-15 minutes until well risen and golden brown.

8. Cool on a wire rack if you can resist eating them before that!

A simple recipe that children could do to encourage them to enjoy cooking.

97. *Wholemeal Chelsea Buns*

Makes 14-16 buns

Ingredients:
1 lb (450 g) wholemeal flour
4 oz (110 g) raw cane sugar
1 oz (25 g) fresh yeast or
  the dried equivalent
8 fl oz (225 ml) tepid milk
  (cow's, goat's or soya)

a good pinch of ruthmol
4 oz (110 g) vegetable fat
6 oz (175 g) currants
2 oz (50 g) mixed peel

Method

1. Place the tepid milk in a bowl, add the yeast and teaspoon of sugar. Leave to foam in a warm place for 15-20 minutes.

2. Place the flour in a large mixing bowl (try to keep a constant heat in the room as this ensures a good rise). Rub in 3 (75 g) of the 4 oz (110 g) of vegetable fat. Add the ruthmol and 2 oz (50 g) of the sugar.

3. Add the yeast mixture and knead well for 5 minutes. Then return to the bowl to double in size. This will take between 30 and 40 minutes.

4. To make the buns: make the dough into a rectangle 18" x 12" (45 cm x 30 cm).

5. Dot with the 1 oz (25 g) of vegetable fat and sprinkle the rest of the sugar and fruit evenly on top.

6. Roll up into a long sausage, seam side down.

7. Cut into 14-16 even sized buns and place on a greased baking tray close together to obtain the traditional effect.

8. Allow to prove. Cover with a greased plastic bag until well risen.

9. Bake in an oven at Gas Mark 6, 200°C, 400°F, for 20-30 minutes.

10. Pull apart when cool otherwise they go very dry on the outsides.

98. *Fresh Fruit Salad*

Serves 4

Ingredients:
1 apple - red
1 apple - green
1 orange
1 pear
4 oz (110 g) black and green grapes
1 lemon

Syrup:
½ pt (275 ml) liquid either water
    or orange juice
2 oz (50 g) raw cane sugar
3-4 mint leaves

Other additions when in season:
strawberries, cherries, apricots, plums

Method
1. *Prepare the syrup* by dissolving the sugar in the liquid over a gentle heat. Add the mint leaves and then leave for ½ hour for the subtle flavour to infuse. Pour into a bowl.

2. *Prepare the fruit*: Wash and discard any peel, core, etc. Chop into "bite size" pieces.

3. Place the fruit in the syrup.

4. Squeeze out the juice from the lemon and pour over the fruit.

5. Leave in the fridge for at least ½ hour to chill.

99. *Fruity Jack*

Makes lots!

Ingredients:

7 oz (200 g) rolled oats
4 oz (110 g) vegetable
  margarine
8 oz (225 g) syrup or
  maple syrup

4 oz (110 g) raw cane sugar
2 oz (50 g) chopped raisins

Method

1.   Melt the vegetable margarine, syrup and raw cane sugar in a medium sized saucepan. Do not allow to boil.

2.   Add the chopped raisins.

3.   Stir in the oats.

4.   Grease a shallow tin about 10″ x 6″ (25 cm x 15 cm) and press the mixture in to a thickness of ¼″ (5 mm).

5.   Bake for 30 minutes at Gas Mark 4, 180°C, 350°F, until firm but not brown.

6.   Cut into squares whilst still warm and remove when cool.

Excellent for packed meals and picnics.

Rather sweet, so not something you should eat too much of!

100. *Malt-House Cherry Cake*

The name malt-house comes from the type of flour used. It is a finely ground wholemeal flour of which a small percentage is made up with grains of wheat which have been roasted in malt to give a granary-type flour.

Ingredients:

8 oz (225 g) malt-house flour *or* granary + 2 level teaspoons of baking powder (mix together thoroughly)

2 oz (50 g) vegetable margarine

2 oz (50 g) raw cane sugar

1 tablesp. pure vanilla

2 eggs, size 2 and

1 tablespoon of water

8 oz (225 g) whole glacé cherries

Method

1. Rub the fat into the flour mixture and stir in the sugar and cherries.

2. Beat the eggs and water together in a separate bowl, add the vanilla.

3. Add the liquid and mix using a metal spoon for 1 minute.

4. Line a 1-1½ lb (450-700 g) loaf tin.

5. Turn the mixture into the prepared tin and spread using a knife.

6. Bake at Gas Mark 4, 180°C, 350°F for 30-40 minutes until well risen and golden brown.

7. Allow to cool in the tin.

Better eaten the next day as the crust softens and the flavour develops.

Excellent for packed lunches and picnics

Miscellaneous

101. *Lemon Squash*

Makes approximately 2 pints

Ingredients:
3 large lemons
1½ oz (40 g) citric acid
2½ lb (1 kg 125 g) raw cane sugar

1¼ pts (720 ml) boiling water
¼ pt (150 ml) cold water

Method
1.   Chop up the lemons into small pieces.

2.   Liquidise using ¼ pint (150 ml) of cold water. Turn into a 2½ pt (1.4 litre) heat-proof bowl or jug.

(Lemons that have been frozen, perhaps bought when cheaper in the shops, then allowed to thaw, have skins that are much softer and will liquidise more easily.)

3.   Add the sugar and citric acid to the lemon mixture and pour on the boiling water.

4.   Leave for 12 hours for the flavour of the lemon to be extracted. Then strain.

The squash should then be poured into clean and dry screw top bottles and labelled with the dates, as it should be consumed within fourteen days of making.

102. *Home-made Peanut Butter*

Makes approximately 1¼ lb (560 g)

Ingredients:
1 lb (450 g) peanuts, complete with
   skins, unroasted and unsalted
4 tablesp. soya oil

2 teasp. sesame seed oil
1 teasp. sugar

Method

1. Place the peanuts on a baking sheet and remove any bad nuts.

2. Pour over 2 of the tablespoons of oil and place in the middle of a moderate oven Gas Mark 4, 180°C, 350°F, for 30 minutes until they are golden brown.

3. Allow to cool slightly.

4. Place in a liquidiser with the 2 remaining tablespoons of oil and the sesame seed oil and sugar.

5. Blend until you have the desired consistency.

You can make it coarse, medium or smooth, depending on your own personal preference. If too dry add a little more oil.

Store in clean jars with a lid. I find it is better when kept in the fridge: where it will keep for up to 3 months.

103. *Tropical Muesli*

Serves 3-4

Ingredients:
6 oz (175 g) rolled oats – coarse
2 tablesp. bran
2 oz (50 g) dried pineapple
2 oz (50 g) dried nectarines
2oz (50 g) dried papaw

2 oz (50 g) muscovado sugar
1 oz (25 g) chopped almonds
Enough milk to mix to give
    a smooth consistency

Method
1.   Mix the dried fruits and sugar together. Add the milk and leave. (This muesli is best started the night before.)

2.   Next morning, add all the other ingredients and a little more milk.

3.   Serve in individual bowls.

An exotic variation of the much enjoyed traditional muesli.

104. *Lemon and Carrot Salad*

Serves 4-6 portions

Ingredients:
1-1½ lb (450-750 g) fresh carrots
  – trimmed and washed
2 lemons

1 teaspoon dill seed
1 tablespoon parsley

Method
1.   Simply grate the carrot very finely and place in a serving bowl.

2.   Squeeze the juice from the lemon and pour over the carrot.

3.   Mix in the dill seed and parsley.

4.   Chill thoroughly and decorate with lemon wedges.

Excellent in the summer with any dish and good in the winter for those extra vitamins.

105. *Apple Cheese*

Makes approximately 3¼ lbs of apple cheese

Ingredients:
3 lbs apples – windfalls will do
1 pint (570 ml) of water
1 pint (570 ml) of sweet cider

raw cane sugar (approximately
¾ lb (350 g) to every 1 lb (450 g)
of pulp)
½ teaspoon of allspice

Method

1.   Wash and trim the fruit. Any damaged areas must be removed. Cut into quarters and place in a preserving pan.

2.   Add the water and sweet cider.

3.   Simmer until the fruit is softened. Cool slightly, then liquidise, then sieve. Discard the residue.

4.   Weigh the pulp and allow ¾ lb (350 g) of sugar to every one pound of pulp.

5.   Place the pulp in a preserving pan and simmer so as to reduce the moisture content which will give a thick consistency.

6.   Add the sugar and allspice stirring well until *NO* free liquid remains.

7.   Pour into clean, hot jars and seal at once. Store in a cool place and use within 6 weeks.

If your family are like mine then this will hardly last 2 weeks, never mind six. Delicious on bread, scones or Welsh cakes.

MILK-FREE RECIPES

A Cow's Milk free diet

Being allergic to cow's milk will not only mean giving up your daily pinta, but also becoming an avid reader of all the packeted goods you purchase and intend to eat. You will have to avoid all products which state they contain any of the following:

Lacto proteins	whey powder	skimmed milk powder
Lactic acid	caseinate or	
Lactose	sodium caseinate	

You will find that on visits to the supermarket you will build up a personal list of foods to avoid, but to help you on your way I have produced a list below:

1. Check all sausages except the 100% meat variety (e.g. Marks & Spencer's). You may be lucky to find a butcher who will make you up a batch of rusk free sausages. Although expensive, you will need a freezer in which to store them, a worthwhile investment for quick meals.

2. All beefburgers except those you make yourself, or the 100% beef variety.

3. Most patés, whether tinned, packeted or bought by the ounce. See list above for ingredients to avoid. Some do not contain milk products so hunt through.

4. Most fish products that are coated in breadcrumbs or batter.

5. Any dairy preparations e.g. ice-cream, frozen desserts, etc.

6. Check sweets as many contain whey powder or skimmed milk.

7. All milk chocolate, chocolate products except those made from plain chocolate . Check the fillings, for bars, sweets etc. may be plain on the outside but have milk included in their fillings.

8. Some prepared breakfast cereals have milk products added to them.

9. Most margarine with the exception of Vitaquell, Vitasieg or Kosher margarine as most others contain milk products.

N.B. Check with your doctor or homoeopath as to whether you are

110

allowed butter, as each person shows a different kind of response to the by-products of milk.

You must also check whether you are allergic to cheese. If not, you may be allowed vegetarian cheese which differs from ordinary cheese in that it is made from non animal rennet extracted from a French mushroom and so does not set off an allergic response. This will also allow you to eat a greater variety of foods. Failing this, you can purchase goat's cheese which is perhaps an acquired taste, but can be put into other dishes to give a varied texture and flavour.

Alternative types of milk are:
1. Goat's milk
You will find this in most health food shops, often frozen, as it remains fresh for only 1-2 days. If you find that one particular type is unpalatable try another as goat's milk differs so much. It depends on the time of year, what the goat is being fed on, and the actual breed of the goat. So don't give up – it took me nearly 10 months to find the type which I now enjoy the most.

You will aslo find goat's milk yoghurt which comes in natural as well as fruit flavoured cartons. This is excellent as a topping as well as for the enjoyment of eating it by itself. It can also be used in desserts to give body to cheese cakes and mousses.

2. Soya milk
This is available on the market in most health food shops.

Granose, packeted
It comes plain or flavoured with carob. It has added raw cane sugar and sea salt. I personally find this the most palatable and versatile to use in cooking. It gives a very light texture to scones and batters.

Canned plamil
This is a soya milk made from soya protein and sunflower oil which has to be diluted before use. You should only dilute the amount you need to use as dilution reduces its keeping qualities. This type is particularly useful in the making of sauces, mousses etc. as it has a thick, creamy texture. Plamil also produce a substitute for cream which is called delice which is made from sunflower oil, protein and natural vanilla. It is very useful to use as a topping on fruit and desserts, but is not too successful in other ways e.g. filling a sponge cake.

Plamil make other non animal products. They are rice pudding, Carob-ean (a soya and carob beverage) and pease pudding. Their address is Plamil Foods Ltd., Plamil House, Bowles Well Garden, Folkestone, Kent.

A point to remember is that soya milk will curdle the same as ordinary milk so that the same storage requirements are needed e.g. place in a fridge *un*covered.

5. *Sheep's milk*

Available from Food Watch (*see* p. 146) but to personal callers only. A new product on the market which I myself have only tried once, but if you need yet another alternative milk it is comforting to know that it is available.

It is also possible to purchase sheep's cheese; although supplies are irregular and hard to find you may be lucky enough to find it locally.

6. *Buttermilk*

The liquid that is left over in the butter making process can be used in cooking or drunk. Not readily available. I often mix with fruit and liquidise to give a nutritious drink

Milk-free – A week's planned menu

	Breakfast	Lunch	Tea/Supper
Monday	Cleansing breakfast: juice of 1 lemon in a glass of warm water 1 bowl of muesli fresh juice	Persian lamb kebabs boiled brown rice mixed salad of tomato, cucumber and goat's yoghurt Apple amber	Boiled egg and toast fresh fruit
Tuesday	poached egg on toast fresh juice	Oven baked fish with herbs boiled potatoes a selection of freshly cooked vegetables fresh fruit	Spiced tomato soup toast fresh fruit
Wednesday	Muesli with goat's milk fresh juice	8 oz (225 g) grilled meat, e.g. steak, pork chops Bean sprout salad 2-3 chocolate wholemeal biscuits	The Empress's Salad 2-3 slices of wholemeal bread fresh fruit juice
Thursday	2 rashers of grilled bacon and tomato wholemeal bread juice	Shepherd's pie mixed vegetables fresh fruit	Salmon paté à la maison wholemeal bread Bengal chutney fresh fruit
Friday	half a grapefruit boiled egg and soldiers juice	Sunshine chicken Ravigote bread Melting moments juice	pancakes filled with peaches, banana and prunes 1 slice of date and walnut loaf juice
Saturday	beans on toast juice	Spanish omelette fresh fruit	Rata bourguignon jacket potatoes, green beans Chocolate and orange mousse juice
Sunday	muesli with goat's milk juice	Barbecued pork with black bean sauce boiled brown rice with sweetcorn green salad Apricot and almond whip apple juice	Cheese scones, buttered Quick lime mousse Tropical fruit cake lemon tea

MILK-FREE RECIPES

Starters

106. Cold Summer Ratatouille
107. Hot Ravigote Bread
108. Spiced Tomato Soup
109. Salmon Paté à la maison
110. Avocado and Tofu Dip
111. Quick Melon cups
112. Hearty Leek and Potato Soup

Main Courses

113. Persian Lamb Kebabs
114. Chili con Carne with Colorado Sauce
115. Sweet and Sour Pork
116. Italian Liver
117. Bean Sprout Salad
118. Oven baked fish with herbs
119. Spanish Omelette
120. Rata Bourguignon
121. Sunshine Chicken
122. Barbecued Pork with Black Bean Sauce
123. Grandmother's Pôtée
124. The Empress's Salad

Sweets

125. Shrewsbury biscuits
126. Brandy Snaps
127. Cheese Scones (made with vegetarian or goat's cheese)
128. Melting Moments
129. Bread and Butter Pudding
130. Chocolate and Orange Mousse
131. Florentines
132. Chocolate Wheatmeal Biscuits
133. Pancakes
134. Tropical Fruit Cake
135. Date and Walnut Loaf
136. Apricot and Almond Whip

Miscellaneous

137. Muesli
138. Bengal chutney
139. Mushroom ketchup
140. Spicy tomato sauce
141. Pomello marmalade
142. Honey Cup (a night cap)
143. Fluffy Cream-like Topping

Starters

106. *Cold Summer Ratatouille*

Serves 4

Ingredients:

2 fresh tomatoes	2 onions
1 medium aubergine	2 cloves of garlic
1 red pepper	a bunch of parsley, chopped
1 green pepper	3 tablesp. vegetable oil
3 courgettes	black pepper

Method

1. Wash and clean all the vegetables.

2. Remove excess water by draining.

3. Slice the onions, aubergines, tomatoes, peppers and courgettes.

4. Heat the oil gently and add the onions. Stir and cook for 2 minutes.

5. Add all the other ingredients and heat through.

6. Place in a moderate oven, Gas Mark 4, 180°C, 350°F, for 1½ hours until cooked. The vegetables should be tender but not mushy.

7. Place in individual dishes – ramekins will do – and chill thoroughly. Sprinkle with more chopped parsley before serving. Serve with hot ravigote bread (*see* below).

107. *Hot Ravigote Bread*

You first have to make ravigote butter and to do this you:

1. Take a heaped tablespoon of the following:
   tarragon, parsley, chives, chervil and one clove of garlic

2. Wash the herbs, peel the garlic and chop until *very* fine.

3. Soften 3-4 oz (75-110 g) of vegetable fat or butter and mix in the prepared herbs.

115

4.   Cut a small loaf into slices and spread with the ravigote butter.

5.   Reassemble the loaf and cover with foil and place in a low oven Gas Mark ¼, 110°C, 225°F, for 20 minutes to allow the flavours to mingle and the loaf to become crusty on the outside.

6.   Serve on a warm serving dish with the cold summer ratatouille.

N.B. The ravigote butter mixture is excellent to fry croutons in – which can then be served with a delicate flavoured soup e.g. cream of celery, hearty leek and potato soup.

108. *Spiced Tomato Soup*

Serves

Ingredients:
2 large onions – chopped
1 oz (25 g) vegetable fat
2 lb (900 g) unskinned tomatoes
2 pts (1 litre 150 ml) stock
   (meat or vegetable)
1 teasp. paprika
1 oz (25 g) flour – white
   or wholemeal

1 large glass of port or sherry
bouquet garni (*see Cookery
Terms*: p. 6)
3 strips of lemon peel
ruthmol and black pepper
1 teasp. raw cane sugar
2 oz (50 g) small pasta shapes –
   ready cooked

Method
1.   Melt the vegetable fat and add the chopped onions. Cook until soft.

2.   Add the flour and make a roux, mixing thoroughly to ensure that all the lumps are removed.

3.   Add the tomatoes, lemon peel, stock, paprika, bouquet garni and seasoning and sugar.

4.   Stir until the mixture boils, then reduce the heat and simmer for 45 minutes.

5.   Remove the bouquet garni and lemon peel.

6.   Sieve or blend. Reheat and then add the ready cooked small pasta shapes, and port or sherry. Do not re-boil or this will impair the delicious flavour.

Serve at once.

109. *Salmon Paté à la maison*

Serves

Ingredients:
7½ oz (210 g) tin red salmon
2 oz (50 g) wholemeal breadcrumbs
2 oz (50 g) melted vegetable margarine
½ level teasp. grated lemon rind
juice of ½ lemon

1 small onion – grated
2 tablesp. dry sherry
1 egg, size 3, beaten
pinch of mace
ruthmol and black pepper

Method
1.   Remove bones and skin from the salmon and mash in a mixing bowl.

2.   Add all remaining ingredients and beat mixture until smooth.

3.   Line a 1½ pt (850 ml) terrine or loaf tin with foil. Pour in the mixture and smooth the surface and cover with foil.

4.   Bake at Gas Mark 3, 170°C, 325°F for 1¼ hours or until firm and set.

Leave in tin until cold.

To serve: Shred a lettuce and place on an oval serving dish. Place the paté on top of the lettuce and arrange thin slices of cucumber down the middle. Slice a tomato into wedges and place on top of the lettuce.

110. *Avocado and Tofu Dip*

Serves 4

Ingredients:
1 large ripe avocado	ruthmol
5 oz (125 g) fresh tofu	black pepper
1 tablesp. tomato sauce	2 cloves of garlic –
2 teasp. cider vinegar	crushed

Method

1. Peel and stone the avocado, mash it until smooth in a bowl using a fork. Add the tomato sauce, tofu, vinegar, ruthmol, pepper and crushed garlic.

2. Mix together thoroughly.

3. Turn the dip into a medium sized bowl.

Serve with finger of vegetables e.g. celery, spring onion, cucumber, radish, apple, green pepper.

This dip is ideal as a starter or as part of a buffet meal.

111. *Quick Melon Cups*

Serves 4
A quick refreshing drink, decorated with melon balls, to serve either
as a starter to a meal or as a refreshing drink.

Ingredients:	*Equipment*:
1 small red melon, watermelon	1 melon baller
(or ¼ of a large one)	4 tall glasses
1 small lemon	4 cocktail sticks
1 small orange	
4 sprigs mint	
1 oz (25 g) raw cane sugar	

Method
1.   Cut the melon and make 8 melon balls, taking care to make sure
that they are well shaped. Put the balls to one side.

2.   Chop the melon into large chunks and place in a Moulinex grinder
and squash through using a bowl to catch the juice. (A sieve and
wooden spoon would also be suitable if no grinder is available.)

3.   Take the tall glasses and dip them into water and then dip them in
the sugar.

4.   Pour the prepared watermelon juice into the tall glasses. Cut the
orange and lemon into thin slices – you will need 8 orange slices and 4
lemon slices. Then thread the melon balls and lemon and orange slices
onto the cocktail sticks and pop on top of the glasses.

This is a drink I first tasted whilst on holiday in Iran, where I
attended a wedding at which it was served.

112. *Hearty Leek and Potato Soup*

Serves 4

Ingredients:
2 lb (900 g) potatoes – peeled
  and diced
2 oz (50 g) vegetable margarine
8 oz (225 g) leeks – trimmed,
  washed and chopped
1 oz (25 g) flour (white or wholemeal) – if required

¼ pt (150 ml) soya milk
2 pt (1.1 litres) stock or water
  (vegetable water will do)
2 teasp. ruthmol
a good pinch of black
  pepper

Method

1.   Melt the vegetable margarine and sauté the potatoes and leeks until soft, but not brown.

2.   Add the stock, salt and pepper. Bring to the boil and simmer until the vegetables are thoroughly cooked.

3.   Cool slightly, and pass through a liquidiser or sieve. (If you use a sieve remember to remove the pulp from the under side of the sieve.)

4.   Blend the flour with the milk and add to the purée. Bring back to the boil stirring well.

Serve piping hot with pieces of toast.

Main Courses

113. *Persian Lamb Kebabs*

Serves 4

Ingredients:

1½ lb (675 g) lamb chopped into cubes about 1″ square (good quality meat should be used e.g. leg of lamb).

The following spices mixed together in a large bowl:

½ teasp. ground ginger	½ teasp. black pepper
1 teasp. garlic – pressed	1 teasp. ruthmol or salt
1½ teasp. red pepper	pinch of nutmeg
½ teasp. turmeric	pinch of mace
1 teasp. poppy seed	6 cloves
½ teasp. cumin seed	1 large carton of goat's milk
1 teasp. coriander seed	natural yoghurt
¼ teasp. green cardamom	*½ cucumber – peeled and diced

Method

1.   Mix all the spices together in the large bowl, blend in the goat's milk yoghurt until well mixed.

2.   Add the cubed meat ensuring all the meat is coated in the yoghurt sauce.

3.   Leave for 24 hours for the flavours to permeate the meat.

4.   *Next day*: Put the meat onto kebab sticks and cook either on a barbecue or under the grill, turning to ensure even cooking: (a barbecue does give that extra flavour and is excellent for a summer party.)

Serve on a bed of brown long grain rice with a yoghurt dressing and cucumber sauce served separately. Cook 3 oz (75 g) rice per person, boiling in an ample amount of water with a teaspoon of salt.

*See *Egg-free* section for yoghurt and cucumber sauce under *Salad Dressing*.

114. *Chili con Carne with Colorado Sauce*

Serves 4-6

Ingredients:
Colorado sauce

6-7 chilies
1 red pepper
Liquidise to give a red slush-like mixture

1 large onion
2 cloves of garlic

1¼ lb (560 g) minced beef
1 clove of garlic
1 medium onion
2 tablesp. tomato purée
1 teasp. raw cane sugar

Bean preparation
6 oz (175 g) red kidney beans
  (soaked overnight)
1 medium onion stuck with
3 cloves
2 cloves of garlic
1 bouquet garni
(*see Cookery Terms*, p. 6)

Method

1.   To prepare the beans place all the ingredients in a saucepan with enough water to cover and bring to the boil for 30 minutes and then simmer for a further 1½ hours. Top up if necessary.

OR

Place in a pressure cooker and cook at 15 lbs pressure for 40-45 minutes.

2.   Brown the meat, onion and garlic in a frying pan and mix in the sugar and tomato purée. Then transfer to a large casserole dish with a lid.

3.   Add the colorado sauce and the bean mixture with enough water to cover.

4.   Place in a moderate oven for 2-2½ hours to allow the flavour to develop at Gas Mark 3, 170°C, 325°F.

This is an original Mexican recipe which is very hot and tasty. If you feel you want a less hot chili con carne reduce the quantity of chili. Serve with a bowl of long grain brown rice mixed with half a tin of sweetcorn.

Excellent dinner party dish – it's always the topic of discussion!

115. *Sweet and Sour Pork*

Serves 3

Ingredients:
½ lb (225 g) pork – cubed (if not cooked, stir fry for 5 minutes)
(Good quality meat should be used e.g. tenderloin, leg)

Batter ingredients
2 teasp. vinegar
2 teasp. soya sauce
½ teasp. ruthmol
1 clove of garlic
½ egg
2 tablesp. wholemeal flour

Sauce ingredients
1 medium green pepper
2 slices of pineapple
2 oz (50 g) cucumber, carrots,
    mushrooms – mixed together
1 heaped tablesp. cornflour
1 teasp. soya sauce
3 teasp. vinegar
3 tablesp. raw cane sugar
6 tablesp. stock e.g. vegetable water

Method
1. Allow the meat to cool before handling if stir fried.

2. Mix the batter ingredients together. Add the cubed meat and coat well.

3. Shallow fat fry until crisp and golden. Drain and keep warm.

4. To make the sauce – sauté the vegetables and pineapple in a little oil until soft.

5. Blend the flour, soya sauce and vinegar until creamy. Add the sugar and stock and add to the vegetables, cooking until the mixture thickens.

6. *To serve*: Place the pork on a bed of long grain brown rice and pour over the delicious sweet and sour sauce.

Eat straight away to enjoy it at its best.

116. *Italian Liver*

Serves 3-4

Ingredients:

1 lb (450 g) lamb's liver
2 medium onions
2 oz (50 g) streaky bacon
4 tablesp. tomato purée
12 oz (350 g) wholemeal or
   buckwheat spaghetti

½ pt (275 ml) vegetable stock
good pinch of ruthmol
2 teasp. oregano
1 bay leaf
2 tablesp. vegetable oil

Method

1.   Trim the liver, removing skin, gristle etc., and cut into slivers 2″ (5 cm) in length.

2.   Peel and slice the onion, chop the bacon.

3.   Heat the oil, add the onions and bacon and cook until soft. Add the liver and cook for a further 5 minutes. Stir well.

4.   Add the stock, tomato purée, ruthmol, oregano and bay leaf and simmer for 45 minutes. If the liquid evaporates a little more may be added.

5.   Cook the spaghetti until tender. Drain and place in a serving bowl.

6.   Pour over the sauce and sprinkle with a little chopped parsley.

Serve immediately.

117. *Bean Sprout Salad*

Serves 4-5

Ingredients:

1 lb (450 g) bean sprouts – blanched
   and cooled
1 bunch of spring onions

Dressing:

2 tablesp. soya sauce
1 tablesp. sesame oil
1 teasp. brown sugar
2 tablesp. wine/cider vinegar

Method
1. Before blanching the bean sprouts ensure that any discoloured sprouts are discarded.
2. Combine all the dressing ingredients together and mix well.
3. Place the blanched and cooled bean sprouts into a serving bowl.
4. Pour over the dressing and toss.
5. Allow to stand for 1 hour in the fridge before serving.

An unusual combination of flavours giving a welcome change to the usual type of side salad.

118. *Oven-baked fish with herbs*

Serves 4

Ingredients:
4 cod fillets
2 oz (50 g) vegetable margarine
1 lemon
bouquet garni – made up of
  2 sprigs of parsley and 1 bay leaf

1 large onion
1 clove of garlic
2 sprigs of thyme

Method
1. Chop the onion and parsley finely.
2. Crush the clove of garlic and add to the onion. Mix together.
3. Take each cod fillet and press the chopped onion mixture onto the fish and roll up.
4. Take an oven proof dish (preferably oblong) and grease the dish using all the margarine. Place the rolled fillets in it carefully.
5. Cover with foil and place in an oven for 30 minutes before the end of cooking to ensure the fish is golden brown.

Garnish with lemon wedges and sprinkle with the fresh thyme.

Serve with potatoes and a selection of fresh vegetables, e.g. french beans, carrots, sautéd mushrooms.

119. *Spanish Omelette*

Ingredients:

3 eggs and 3 teaspoons of water
2 sliced onions
2 sliced tomatoes
1 tablesp. oil
1 tablesp. vinegar

cayenne pepper and ruthmol
pinch of fresh or dried tarragon
Optional extras:
2 oz (50 g) cooked peas
.4 oz (110 g) cooked potatoes

Method

1. Fry the onion and tomato in the oil until tender, but not brown. Add the peas and potatoes if desired.

2. Beat the eggs in a bowl, add the cayenne pepper, ruthmol and tarragon.

3. Pour the egg mixture over the fried ingredients.

4. Lift the edges of the omelette to allow excess egg mixture to flow away.

5. When golden brown on the under side, place under the grill to cook the top of the omelette.

Serve on a warmed plate with a small side salad of crisp lettuce, onion rings and plump tomatoes covered in french dressing.

An excellent meal for its high food value at a relatively low cost.

120. *Rata Bourguignon*

Serves 4

Ingredients:

1 lb (450 g) stewing steak
½ lb (225 g) red peppers
½ lb (225 g) green peppers
2 onions
1 lb (450 g) fresh tomatoes
½ lb (225 g) sliced carrots

1 tablesp. soya oil
2 cloves of garlic – crushed
a good pinch of dried basil
a good pinch of thyme
2 large bay leaves
ruthmol and cayenne pepper

½-¾ pt (275-425 ml) water or stock – a little red wine may be used if available.
(A heavy oven proof iron casserole dish is ideal for this dish)

Method

1. Trim the meat and cut into 1″ (2.5 mm) cubes.

2. Heat the soya oil and seal the meat for 4-6 minutes, then add the onions, garlic, basil and thyme and bay leaves and cook for a further 5 minutes. Then add the ruthmol and liquid.

3. Wash the vegetables and shred the peppers into ½″ (1 cm) by 2″-3″ (5-7 .5 cm) strips, slice the onions and carrots and finally cut the tomatoes into quarters. Add to the casserole dish and continue cooking for a further 15 minutes.

4. Put in an oven at Gas Mark 3, 170°C, 325°F for 2-2¾ hours until the meat is tender and the vegetables are soft.

Serve with freshly boiled potatoes and a crisp green salad. I feel this recipe gives a new interpretation of two traditional French dishes.

121. *Sunshine Chicken*

Serves 4-6

Ingredients:

1 roasted chicken, weighing 3-3½ lbs
8-10 oz (225-275 g) brown rice – cooked
8 oz (225 g) can of sweetcorn
1 small can of butterbeans
(or 4 oz (110 g) dried butterbeans,
soaked overnight and then boiled
for 40 minutes until tender)

4 sticks of celery – diced
1 medium green pepper – diced
1 orange
1 bunch of water cress – washed

Method

1. Having roasted the chicken strip all the meat from the bone and chop into ½″ (1 cm) cubes. Place in the fridge.

2. Boil the rice using the stock from the chicken and enough water to cover the rice for 20-25 minutes until tender. Drain, then allow to cool.

3. Using a large bowl put in the sweetcorn, butter beans, diced celery and pepper and mix. Then add the cooled rice and the chicken and mix all the ingredients thoroughly together.

4.   Take a large bowl 9-10″ (23-25 cm) in diameter and place the watercress around the edges. Carefully place the chicken mixture in the centre.

5.   Peel the orange removing the skin and peel. Keep in segments and arrange in a circle to represent the sun shining.

---

122. *Barbecued pork with black bean sauce*

Serves 4-6

Ingredients:
2 lb (900 g) pork – a joint that you would normally roast would be ideal e.g. leg, tender loin
3 tablesp. Hoi-Sin sauce
2 tablesp. black beans – these can be purchased from most Chinese supermarkets in a tin. They are salty with an exotic taste.

3 tablesp. soya oil
¼ pt (150 ml) water
2 teasp. cornflour – blended with a little water

A selection of vegetables to cook with the meat e.g. tomatoes, green peppers, shallots, allowing 1 tomato, 2 shallots and half a green pepper per person.

Method
1.   Remove the fat from the meat and cut into cubes. Place in a bowl.

2.   Add one tablespoon of the soya oil, the Hoi-Sin sauce and black beans and leave for 1-2 hours until the meat has absorbed the flavour.

3.   Thread onto skewers and place on a preheated barbecue. Cook for 30 minutes until very well done. Use the two remaining tablespoons of oil to baste the meat during cooking as this stops the meat from becoming too dry.

4.   Keep the juice from meat and place in a saucepan. Heat, add the water and the blended cornflour and cook gently until the sauce is thickened, stirring continuously.

Serve with the barbecued vegetables and a green salad. To make a complete Sunday lunch serve with melon cup for starters and Apricot and Almond Whip for dessert.

This is a nutritional meal that almost anyone can enjoy.

123. *Grandmother's Pôtée*

Serves

Ingredients:
2 lb (900 g) shoulder of ham
1 lb (450 g) spicy sausages
½ lb (225 g) beans – flageolets

1 lb (450 kg) potatoes
1-1¼ lb (450-560 g) white cabbage
seasoning: thyme and pepper

Method
1.   Prepare the beans the night before. Soak in cold water.

2.   Take a large casserole dish and put the ham and beans in. Add enough water to cover the meat and simmer for ½ hour.

3.   Prepare the cabbage by blanching in boiling water for 5-7 minutes.

4.   Cut it into quarters and add to the casserole dish. Simmer for a further ½ hour. Season to taste.

5.   Add the sausages and the potatoes and simmer for another ½ hour. (The pôtée should be simmered for about 1½ hours in all.) It is not necessary to add any salt as the ham makes the complete dish sufficiently salty.

To serve: Day 1
You eat the sausages and only one slice of the ham per person with the cabbage, potatoes and beans.

To serve: Day 2

You serve the liquid as a clear soup with toasted wholemeal bread, and eat the remaining ham cold with either a salad or freshly cooked vegetables.

N.B. Sometimes the ham is rather salty, so simply place the ham in a saucepan, add cold water to cover and bring to the boil. Then discard the liquid. This will ensure your pôtée is correctly seasoned.

This is a traditional French dish, both economical and wholesome. It is simple, nutritious and very tasty. It originates from the north of Brittany where there is a large farming community and where the ingredients of the pôtée are found in abundance.

---

124. *The Empress's Salad*

Serves 4

Ingredients:
1 small can of sweetcorn
1 medium sized orange – peeled
1 ripe mango – peeled
1 William pear – peeled
1 ripe avocado – peeled

1 small fresh pineapple – peeled
4 oz (110 g) black grapes – washed
1 small red chili – washed and
   diced into very small pieces
lettuce and parsley to garnish

Dressing:
4 tablesp. soya oil

1 tablesp. cider vinegar

Method

1. Slice the mango, pear and pineapple making the pieces even.

2. Take the peeled orange and cut into segments removing any excess pith.

3. The avocado should be made into small balls. If you don't have a "baller" use a teaspoon.

4. Wash and dry the lettuce and arrange around the edge of a shallow salad bowl.

5. Fill the centre of the bowl with the fruit and top with the sweetcorn, grapes and chopped chili.

6. Prepare the dressing by mixing the oil and vinegar together and pour over the prepared salad.

To complete: Sprinkle with chopped parsley and chill for 30 minutes before serving.

Sweets

125. *Shrewsbury biscuits*

Ingredients:
8 oz (200 g) wholemeal flour
4 oz (100 g) vegetable margarine
4 oz (100 g) caster sugar

1 egg yolk
rind of 1 lemon

Method
1. Cream the fat and sugar together, then beat in the egg yolk.

2. Add the lemon rind and flour.

3. Knead well until smooth.

4. Roll out to ¼" (5 mm) thick.

5. Cut out and place on a greased baking tray. (Traditionally they should be 5" (13 cm) in diameter.) Prick well.

6. Bake for 15-20 minutes at Gas Mark 4, 180°C, 350° F. Dredge with raw cane caster sugar whilst still warm.

126. *Brandy snaps*

Ingredients:
2 tablesp. syrup
2 oz (50 g) wholemeal flour
2 oz (50 g) raw cane sugar
2 oz (50 g) vegetable margarine,
  butter or lard

½ teasp. lemon rind
1 teasp. lemon juice
1 level teasp. ground ginger

Method
1. Melt the fat, add the sugar and syrup. *Warm* gently.

2. Stir in the flour, ginger and lemon rind and juice.

3. Drop small teaspoons of the mixture onto a baking sheet well apart. (No more than 5-6 per tin measuring 8" x 10" (20cm x 25 cm).)

4. Bake for 8-10 minutes at Gas Mark 3, 170°C, 325°F; allow to cool for only a moment or two. Then lift off the baking tray using a palette knife and loosely roll round a wooden spoon handle. Serve with coffee or cold drinks or with stewed fruit as a dessert.

127. *Cheese scones*

Makes 6-8

Ingredients:

8 oz (225 g) wholemeal flour
3 heaped teasp. baking powder
2 oz (50 g) vegetable fat or butter
salt and pepper
¼ pt (150 ml) goat's milk

2 tomatoes
2 oz (50 g) vegetarian cheese or
    goat's cheese
    (If you are not allergic to
    ordinary cheese use that)

Method

1. Sieve the baking powder and flour together.

2. Rub in the fat, add the cheese, salt and pepper.

3. Add the milk all at once and using a rounded knife mix to form a soft dough.

4. Gently knead and roll out to ½″ (1 cm) thickness and cut out.

5. Place on a well greased baking sheet and bake at the top of the oven for 12-15 minutes at Gas Mark 7, 220°C, 425°F. Cool. Split open, butter and put slices of tomato on the top and serve.

128. *Melting moments*

Makes 12

Ingredients:

4 oz (110 g) vegetable margarine
    or butter
4 oz (110 g) raw cane caster sugar
1 egg

6 oz (175 g) self-raising flour
    (can be white or wholemeal with
    1 teasp. baking powder)
2 oz (50 g) rolled oats

Method

1. Cream the fat and sugar together until light and fluffy.

2. Add the egg and then the flour.

3. The dough should be stiff enough to handle. If not add a little more flour.

4. Using wet hands divide the mixture into 24 equal sized balls.

5.   Roll the balls in the rolled oats and place on a greased baking tray, allowing sufficient space for spreading during cooking.

6.   Place in the middle to top part of a pre-heated oven for 20 minutes at Gas Mark 4, 180°C, 350°F.

7.   Allow to stand on the baking tray for 2-3 minutes to allow to set before transferring to a cooling tray.

Store in an airtight tin.

Excellent for packed lunches or picnics.

129. *Bread and butter pudding*

Serves 4

Ingredients:
6 medium slices wholemeal bread
3-4 oz (75-110 g) currants
2 oz (50 g) vegetable fat or butter
2 eggs

2 oz (50 g) raw cane sugar
½ pt (275 ml) goat's milk
sprinkling of nutmeg or
   allspice

Method
1.   Grease a 2 pt oven proof dish.

2.   Spread butter on the bread and sandwich together. Place half the bread in the dish.

3.   Sprinkle over the sugar and fruit and cover with the remaining bread.

133

4.   Beat the egg in a separate bowl, add the milk gradually. Strain the custard over the bread.

5.   Sprinkle with nutmeg or allspice.

6.   Leave for 14 minutes for the milk to soak into the bread.

7.   Bake in the middle of the oven for 20-30 minutes at Gas Mark 3, 170°C, 325°F, ensuring that the custard is set and the top of the pudding is crisp and brown.

Serve hot or cold.

130. *Chocolate and orange mousse*

Serves 2-4

Ingredients:

4-6 oz (110-175 g) plain chocolate or carob chocolate substitute

1 teasp. coffee

1 tablesp. orange juice

2 teasp. brandy or orange liqueur (optional)

3 eggs, size 2 – separated

Method

1.   Put the chocolate in a large bowl over hot water and leave until soft.

2.   Add the coffee, orange juice and egg yolks and beat with a whisk until the mixture thickens slightly. Ensure that the bowl does not *touch* the hot water.

3.   Remove from the heat and allow to cool slightly.

4.   Add the brandy (optional).

5.   Beat the egg whites until stiff and fold into the chocolate mixture using a metal spoon.

6.   Turn into a glass bowl and chill for 2 hours.

Excellent to complete a dinner party on a warm summer's evening.

131. *Florentines*

Makes 8-10

Ingredients:

2 oz (50 g) vegetable fat or butter
2 oz (50 g) raw cane sugar
1 dessert spoon honey
2 oz (50 g) candied peel

1 oz (25 g) glacé cherries
1 oz (25 g) blanched almonds
2 oz (50 g) flour (white or whole-meal)
2 oz (50 g) plain chocolate

Method

1. Cover 3 baking trays with oiled paper – greaseproof will do.

2. Melt the fat in a small pan, add the sugar and cook for one minute.

3. Remove from the heat and stir in the nuts, peel, cherries, honey and flour.

4. Drop the mixture in teaspoons onto the oiled paper. Leave room for them to spread during cooking.

5. Bake for 8-10 minutes at Gas Mark 4, 180°C, 350°F.

6. Allow to cool on the paper and peel off when cooled.

7. Spread the underside of the biscuits with melted chocolate and mark wavy lines across them with a fork. Allow to cool.

Delicious with coffee on a Sunday morning or to brighten up a picnic box.

132. *Chocolate wheatmeal biscuits*

Makes 25 biscuits

Ingredients

8 oz (225 g) wheatmeal flour
3 oz (75 g) vegetable margarine or butter
2½ oz (60 g) fructose *or* 4 oz (110 g) raw cane sugar

pinch of ruthmol
1 egg, size 3 or 4
6 oz (175 g) plain chocolate

135

Method

1. Rub the fat into the flour.

2. Stir in the ruthmol and fructose

3. Beat the egg in a separate bowl and add to the flour mixture all at once.

4. Mix using a round ended knife to form a stiff dough.

5. Knead to ensure a smooth dough and allow to relax for 10 minutes in the fridge.

6. Roll out to ¼″ (5 mm) thickness and using a 2″ (5 cm) cutter cut out the biscuits and place on an oiled baking tray. Prick with a fork to make a pattern to stop the biscuits from rising.

7. Bake for 15-18 minutes until cooked at Gas Mark 5-6, 200°C, 400°F.

8. Place on a wire rack to cool.

9. Place chocolate in a bowl over a pan of hot *not* boiling water to melt.

10. Using a knife spread the underside of the biscuits with chocolate and make a pattern using the end of the knife.

11. Allow the chocolate to set completely and then serve.

Delicious and tempting!

---

133. *Pancakes*

Makes 6

Ingredients:

4 oz (110 g) flour (white or
   wholemeal)
1 egg, size 3
½ pt (275 ml) goat's or soya milk

pinch of ruthmol
vegetable oil for frying
sugar and lemon to serve

Method

1. Place the flour in a mixing bowl and add the ruthmol and stir.

2. Make a well in the centre and drop in the egg.

3. Using a wooden spoon mix together, adding the milk slowly. When half the milk is added beat vigorously until the mixture is smooth and shiny.

4. Stir in the remaining milk.

5. Store in the fridge if the mixture is to be used later.

6. Heat a little oil in a frying pan.

7. Pour enough batter into the frying pan to make a thin layer over the base.

8. Cook until lightly brown. Turn over with a palette knife or by tossing and cook the second side until lightly brown.

9. Turn out onto sugared paper and sprinkle with sugar and lemon juice. Roll up. .

10. Arrange several on a warmed serving plate and garnish with slices of lemon.

Serve immediately.

---

134. *Tropical fruit cake*

A very rich cake that needs seven days for the flavours to develop and the texture to become moist. It is a variation of a traditional fruit cake with a new flavour to it, the wholemeal flour giving it a very nutty taste.

Ingredients:

8 oz (225 g) vegetable margarine
8 oz (225 g) raw cane sugar
4 eggs, size 2
10 oz (275 g) wholemeal flour
1½ teasp. baking powder
(mixed together)
6 tablesp. sherry*

4 oz (110 g) chopped prunes
4 oz (110 g) dried pineapple –
   chopped
8 oz (225 g) sultanas
2 oz (50 g) dates
4 oz (100 g) dried bananas

Method
1. Cream the fat and sugar until pale in colour.

2. Beat the eggs in a separate bowl.

3. Add one third of the eggs and beat, add the second third and beat again.

4.   Add 2 tablespoons of flour and the remaining third of the eggs. Heat until thoroughly mixed.

5.   Add all the chopped dried fruit to the flour and mix.

6.   Add the fruit mixture to this 3-4 tablespoons at a time. Continue until all the fruit is added. Give one final thorough mixing.

7.   Line an 8″ (20 cm) square tin with greaseproof paper. A little vegetable oil may be used to ensure that the paper sticks to the the tin.

8.   Put the mixture into the prepared tin. Make a dip in the centre so that the cake remains flat whilst baking.

9.   Place in a pre-heated oven at Gas Mark 3, 170°C, 325°F for 2-2½ hours. Test with a skewer. If the skewer comes out dry the cake is cooked.

Cool in the tin overnight and pop into a plastic bag for 5-7 days; the cake will then be ready to eat.

*Simply pour the sherry over the cake when cool before popping into a plastic bag for 5-7 days.

135. *Date and Walnut Loaf*

Ingredients:
8 oz (225 g) wholemeal flour and
1½ teasp. of baking powder
2 oz (50 g) vegetable margarine
1 oz (25 g) fructose *or* 3 tablesp. honey

2 oz (50 g) chopped walnuts
5 oz (150 g) chopped dates
2 eggs, size 2 and 3 tablesp.
   of cold water

A 1-1½ lb (450-675 g) loaf tin - lined

Method
1.   Mix the flour and baking powder together.

2.   Rub in the fat and then stir in the fructose or honey.

3.   Beat the eggs and water in a separate bowl and stir into the mixture.

4.   Add the chopped walnuts and dates.

5.   Place in the prepared loaf tin and bake for 30-40 minutes at Gas Mark 4, 180°C, 350°F.

Eat the next day - slice and spread with honey.

138

136. *Apricot and Almond whip*

Serves 4-6 portions

Ingredients:
7 oz (200 g) dried apricots
1-1¾ pints (570-720 ml) goat's
    milk natural yoghurt
½ teasp. lemon juice

4 oz (110 g) chopped and toasted
    almonds
1 tablesp. gelatine

Method
1.   *To prepare the gelatine*: dissolve the gelatine in a 2 fluid ounces of cold water using a small bowl. Then put the bowl into a saucepan containing some hot water. This will ensure that the gelatine totally dissolves. If it is still lumpy gently heat the saucepan and stir until dissolved.

2.   Cook the apricots until quite soft - cool and then purée

3.   Beat in the yoghurt, lemon juice and gelatine.

4.   Pour into individual glass dishes and allow to set (between 4-6 hours).

To serve: top with the toasted almonds.

Miscellaneous

137. *Muesli*

Serves 2-4

Ingredients:

3 heaped tablesp. rolled oats
3 heaped tablesp. millet flakes
1 heaped tablesp. bran (optional)
1 heaped tablesp. raisins
1 heaped tablesp. sultanas
1 heaped tablesp. roasted
hazelnuts

1 heaped tablesp. raw cane sugar
2 tablespoons of honey
1 banana – chopped
1 red apple – chopped
Enough goat's milk, goat's milk
natural yoghurt or soya milk to
mix to a soft consistency

Method

1.   Mix all the dry ingredients together in a bowl.

2.   Add enough goat's milk, goat's milk yoghurt or soya milk to make a smooth consistency.

3.   Add the honey and the washed and chopped fruit.

4.   Serve in individual dishes. It may be chilled if preferred.

138. *Bengal chutney*

Makes approx. 4-6 jars

Ingredients:

15 large cooking apples
1 medium onion
1 oz (25 g) garlic – pressed
3 pts (1 litre 700 ml) vinegar
1 oz (25 g) mustard

1 oz (25 g) ground ginger
1 teasp. cayenne pepper
½ lb (225 g) raisins
1 lb (450 g) raw cane sugar
½ teasp. salt or ruthmol

Method

1.   Peel the apples and place in a large pan e.g. preserving pan along with the chopped onion and garlic, and ruthmol.

2.   Add the vinegar and spices and simmer until pulpy.

3. Add the sugar, stir well and continue to cook until all the liquid has disappeared. Care should be taken not to allow the chutney to stick and burn at this stage.

4. Pour into clean, dry jars, seal and label.

This chutney will improve with keeping and is excellent with curries, cheese and cold meats.

As many of the manufactured sauces contain colourings, preservatives, cereals etc., I feel it beneficial to have on hand a recipe or two which will enable you to make your own sauces. Although more expensive to make you are avoiding any of the additives that may upset you.

139. *Mushroom ketchup*

Makes $\frac{3}{4}$ pt (425 ml)

Ingredients:
1½ lb (675 g) mushrooms
½ teasp. pepper
1½ oz (40 g) ruthmol
½ teasp. allspice
pinch of mace

pinch of ginger
pinch of cloves
pinch of cinnamon
½ pt (275 ml) vinegar

Method
1. Chop the mushrooms into small pieces, sprinkle with the ruthmol and leave in a covered bowl overnight.

2. Either mash using a wooden spoon or liquidise (for a short time only).

3. Place in a large saucepan with a lid. Add the vinegar and spices and simmer covered for ½ hour.

4. Pour whilst hot into hot bottles and seal at once.

5. Stand in a pan of hot water and keep this simmering for ½ hour.

6. Label with the date of making and *store in a dark cupboard to preserve the colour*. This ketchup should be consumed within 3-4 months.

141

140. *Spicy tomato sauce*

Makes 1 pint (570 ml)

Ingredients:

1 lb (450 g) ripe tomatoes
½ lb (225 g) cooking apples – unpeeled
4 oz (110 g) raw cane sugar
4 oz (110 g) onions –
peeled and diced
1 teasp. ruthmol

3 cloves
pinch of ground ginger
8 peppercorns
1 chili (optional)
¼ pt (150 ml) cider
vinegar

Method

1.   Wash the apples and tomatoes. Chop and then place in a suacepan.

2.   Add the diced onion.

3.   Simmer in a covered pan using the juice from the tomatoes to prevent burning.

4.   When softened add the vinegar, sugar and spices. Continue simmering in a covered pan for 30 minutes.

5.   Liquidise, then sieve. Return to the pan without the lid on and simmer for 15 minutes to reduce the liquid and so make the sauce thick.

6.   Pour into hot bottles and sterilise by simmering in a water bath for 30 minutes. Seal.

Label and date. This sauce should be used within 3 months of making Delicious and tasty!

141. *Pomello marmalade*

Makes about 5 lbs

Ingredients:

1 pomello
1 grapefruit
1 lemon
2 Seville oranges
(combined weight should
   not exceed 2¾ lbs)

½ oz tartaric acid
3 lbs (1.35 kg) raw cane sugar
2½-2¾ pints (1.4-1.6 litres)
   of water

142

Method

1.   Scrub the fruit, cut into quarters and place in a pressure cooker (without the rack).

2.   Pour in the water, put on the lid and cook using 15 lbs pressure for 20-25 minutes. Allow to cool before handling. (This may be done in a preserving pan, if so, use 5 (2.85 litres) pints of water to cook the fruit in.)

3.   Take the cooked and cooled fruit and remove the flesh from the middle. Then remove the pith and pips and discard. Shred the peel. This does take quite a time to do, so be prepared for this. It may also irritate your hands so it might be wise to wear rubber gloves.

4.   Return the flesh and peel to the pressure cooker (if you find the mixture fills over half the pan then transfer to a preserving pan as when it boils it may come over the sides which is quite dangerous). Add the sugar and bring to the boil using a thermometer. This is the ideal way to make marmalade for it should then reach 220°-221°F. This means that the sugar percentage is right and as long as the pectin and acid proportions are correct then the marmalade will most certainly set (Explanation of the pectin test is at the end of the recipe).

5.   Bring the marmalade to the boil and then boil until you reach 221°F, or until a small amount sets on a saucer.

6.   If you find that your marmalade has a scum on it then add a little vegetable margarine and this should make this scum subside.

7.   Remove from the heat and allow the mixture to cool, then pour into warm and well washed jars.

Place a wax disc on the top, this helps to prevent any moulds from growing on the jam as it will exclude the air and so reduce the risk of

143

the marmalade spoiling. (If you do not allow the marmalade to cool slightly before bottling then most of the peel will settle on the bottom which is not desirable).

8.   Place lids on the jars when cool and label.

A little whisky may be added just before bottling to give the marmalade just an extra *je ne sais quoi*!

Pectin Test

When fruit has simmered and skins are soft follow the Pectin Test :—
1) Take 1 tsp juice, place into a glass and cool.
2) Add 3 tsp methylated spirits, shake gently and leave for one minute.

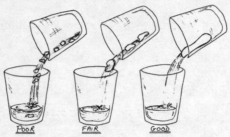

POOR   FAIR   GOOD

3) If plenty of pectin is present a transparent lump will form, if a moderate amount is present the clot will break into 2 or 3, if a small amount is present the clot will break into many pieces.

142. *Honey Cup* (A NIGHT CAP)

Serves 1
Ingredients:
⅓ pint (210 ml) goat's milk
1 heaped teasp. of cocoa

2 heaped teasp. of
clear honey

To garnish:
1 oz (25 g) dried banana chips

Method
1.   Take a mug and place the honey in the bottom.

2. Blend the milk and cocoa and heat until just boiling. Pour onto the honey.

3. Complete by sprinkling the one ounce of banana chips on the surface.

A nourishing drink to end a busy day.

143. *Fluffy Cream-like Topping*

Ingredients:

¾ pt (425 ml) milk (goat's,
   cow's or soya)
4 oz (110 g) cornflour
6 oz (175 g) Vitaquell, unsalted
   butter or vegetable margarine

5 oz (150 g) home made icing sugar
   flavoured with a vanilla pod

Method

1. Blend the cornflour with a little of the milk. Add the remaining milk.

2. Bring slowly to the boil stirring continuously until very thick and smooth. Allow to cool.

3. Beat the fat and icing sugar together until fluffy.

4. Beat the cooled sauce until smooth, then gradually beat in the butter mixture.

Use instead of cream for toppings on puddings, pies and desserts, and for fillings for cakes.

It will keep for 3-4 days covered in the fridge.

SOME USEFUL PEOPLE AND ADDRESSES FOR INFORMATION AND ADVICE
(This is a personal list and in no way comprehensive)

1. Food Watch, High Acre, East Stour, Gillingham Dorset SP8 5JR
   A company which specialises in basic ingredients tailored to meet the needs of those who suffer from food allergies, diabetes and coeliac disease and so require special diets. Their foods are of the highest quality and purity. They also give accurate information about the sources of the food they sell. I find that they have a conscience, do not exploit the public and keep prices stable. A wide range of products is available by mail order; also included are recipes and helpful advice. A wonderful alternative to the mass produced foods, packed with chemicals, so often found in supermarkets and, I am sorry to say, some "health" food shops.
2. Gwynne Davies, "Kaygwynne", Trull Road, Taunton, Somerset
   Writer of the introduction to this book. Will assist individuals in identifying their allergies.
3. Action Against Allergies, "The Downs", Wimbledon, London
   A self-help organisation which assists individuals with their problems.
4. National Child Birth Trust, 9 Queensborough Terrace, London, W2, *Tel*: 01-221 3833
   A national organisation which will assist all mothers with problems concerning their children. Offers breast feeding counsellors who can give sound advice as well as help with practical problems. Look in your telephone directory for your nearest branch.
5. Plamil Foods Ltd., Plamil House, Bowles Well Garden, Folkestone, Kent
   Can be contacted to find out your nearest stockist.

GLOSSARY OF PRODUCTS AVAILABLE

Carob:	Also called the locust bean, this is the fruit of a mediterranean shrub.
Monosodium Glutamate:	An acidic amino acid used widely as a flavour enhancer. Sometimes called Chinese taste powder because the Chinese use it a great deal in cooking.
Fructose:	A natural sugar found in fruit. Useful for diabetics. Twice as sweet as ordinary sugar but rather expensive.

Muesli˙
A combination of cereals, e.g. rolled oats, wheat bran, rye flakes and dried vine fruits, nuts and fresh fruit, made to a smooth consistency with the milk of your choice.

Hoi-Sin Sauce
A combination of fermented soya beans that have been mixed with spices, onions and made into a smooth paste, that can be used to make a barbecue very special or added to grilled meats, or added to casseroles to give them a sweet and spicy flavour.

Rooibosch:
The leaves are dried and used as a substitute for tea. A pleasant flavour.

Ruthmol:
A salt substitute. It is made from potassium chloride and is useful in all types of cooking.

Tomor Margarine:
A kosher product, a milk free block margarine useful for cake making for people who are allergic to cow's milk.

Kosher products:
Products specially prepared for Jewish people. They are extremely reliable products and whatever ingredients are stated on the packet are absolutely correct.

Soya products -
Soya grits:
the soya bean is minced into pieces to enable quicker cooking. Suitable for bean loaf or patties.

T.V.P.:
where the bean is broken and reconstituted by being spun into a meat-like texture. Available in minced or chunk form.

Soya milk:
sold in tins, bottles or spray dried. Soya milk has more iron than cow's milk, but has to be fortified with calcium, phosphorus and Vitamin A.

Tofu:
Soya beans that have been ground and made into an emulsion by the addition of gypsum. Tofu has a soft, delicate texture. Sold in slabs or slices and must be kept in water in the fridge. The Chinese use it in soups or sweetened as a refreshing dessert.

Maple Sugar:
A sugar made by boiling down Maple Syrup. Maple Syrup is made from the sap of the Maple Sugar tree.

Goat's milk:
Often used as a replacement for cow's milk in an allergy diet as it is said not to set up allergic responses in the same way as cow's milk does.

Jaggery: A brown sugar made from palm juice.

Tartrazine: E.E.C. code number 102. An orange dye used to colour many foodstuffs e.g. orange drinks that have to be diluted and ice lollies.

Although at the present moment there is no conclusive evidence to suggest that it is harmful, it is my own personal belief that it may produce side effects such as hyperactivity in children, skin rashes and may also bring on asthmatic attacks, so if you can possibly avoid it then do so!

List of E.E.C Additives

The following is a list of E Numbers and the additives to which they have been assigned by the E.E.C. This list will help you through the additive jungle.

E 100	Curcumin	E 151	Brilliant Black PN
E 101	Riboflavin (lactoflavin)	E 153	Vegetable Carbon (carbon medicinalis vegetalis)
E 102	Tartrazine		
E 104	Quinoline Yellow	E 160	Carotenoids
E 110	Sunset Yellow FCF	E 160a	alpha-, beta- & gamma-carotene
E 120	Carmine (cochineal)		
E 122	Carmoisine	E 160b	Annatto
E 123	Amaranth	E 160c	Capsanthin
E 124	Ponceau 4R	E 160d	Lycopene
E 127	Erythrosine	E 160e	Beta-apo-8'-carotenal
E 128	Red 2G	E 160f	Ethyl ester of beta-apo-8'-carotenal
E 131	Patent Blue V		
E 132	Indigo Carmine	E 161	Xanthophylls
E 133	Brilliant Blue	E 161a	Flavoxanthin
E 140	Chlorophyll	E 161b	Lutein
E 141	Copper complexes of chlorophyll & chlorophyllins	E 161c	Cryptoxanthin
		E 161d	Rubixanthin
		E 161e	Violaxanthin
E 142	Brilliant Green BS (Green S)	E 161f	Rhodoxanthin
		E 161g	Canthaxanthin
E 150	Caramel	E 162	Beetroot Red (Betanin)

E 163	Anthocyanins	E 240	Formaldehyde
E 170	Calcium Carbonate	E 249	Potassium Nitrite
E 171	Titanium Dioxide	E 250	Sodium Nitrite
E 172	Iron Oxides &	E 251	Sodium Nitrate
	Hydroxides	E 252	Potassium Nitrate
E 173	Aluminium	E 260	Acetic Acid
E 174	Silver	E 261	Potassium Acetate
E 175	Gold	E 262	Sodium Diacetate
E 180	Pigment Rubin (Lithol	E 263	Calcium Acetate
	Rubin BK)	E 270	Lactic Acid
E 200	Sorbic Acid	E 280	Propionic Acid
E 201	Sodium Sorbate	E 281	Sodium Propionate
E 202	Potassium Sorbate	E 282	Calcium Propionate
E 203	Calcium Sorbate	E 283	Potassium Propionate
E 210	Benzoic Acid	E 290	Carbon Dioxide
E 211	Sodium Benzoate	E 300	L-Ascorbic Acid
E 212	Potassium Benzoate	E 301	Sodium Ascorbate
E 213	Calcium Benzoate	E 302	Calcium Ascorbate
E 214	Ethyl p-hydroxy	E 303	Ascorbyl Diacetate
	benzoate	E 304	Ascorbyl Palmitate
E 215	Sodium ethyl	E 306	Natural extracts rich in
	p-hydroxybenzoate		tocopherol
E 216	Propyl p-	E 307	Synthetic alpha-
	hydroxybenzoate		tocopherol
E 217	Sodium propyl	E 308	Synthetic beta-
	p-hydroxybenzoate		tocopherol
E 218	Methyl p-	E 309	Synthetic delta-
	hydroxybenzoate		tocopherol
E 219	Sodium methyl	E 310	Propyl Gallate
	p-hydroxybenzoate	E 311	Octyl Gallate
E 220	Sulphur Dioxide	E 312	Dodecyl Gallate
E 221	Sodium Sulphite	E 320	Butylated Hydroxyan-
E 222	Sodium Bisulphite		isole (BHA)
E 223	Sodium Metabisulphite	E 321	Butylated Hydroxyto-
E 224	Potassium Metabisul-		luene (BHT)
	phite	E 322	Lecithins
E 226	Calcium Sulphite	E 325	Sodium Lactate
E 227	Calcium Bisulphite	E 326	Potassium Lactate
E 230	Biphenyl (Diphenyl)	E 327	Calcium Lactate
E 231	Orthophenylphenol	E 330	Citric Acid
E 232	Sodium orthophenyl-	E 331	Sodium Citrates
	phenate	E 332	Potassium Citrates
E 233	Thiabendazole	E 333	Calcium Citrates
E 236	Formic Acid	E 334	Tartaric Acid
E 237	Sodium Formate	E 335	Sodium Tartrates
E 238	Calcium Formate	E 336	Potassium Tartrates
E 239	Hexamethylenetetra-	E 337	Sodium Potassium
	mine		Tartrate

149

E 338	Orthophosphoric Acid	E 460	(i) Microcystalline Cellulose
E 339	Sodium Orthophosphates	E 460	(ii) Powdered Cellulose
E 340	Potassium Orthophosphates	E 461	Methylcellulose
E 341	Calcium Orthophosphates	E 463	Hydroxypropylcellulose
E 342	Calcium Disodium Ethylene Diamine Tetraacetate	E 464	Hydroxypropylmethylcellulose
E 400	Alginic Acid	E 465	Methylethylcellulose
E 401	Sodium Alginate	E 466	Sdium Carboxymethylcellulose
E 402	Potassium Alginate	E 470	Sodium, Potassium & Calcium salts of fatty acids
E 403	Ammonium Alginate		
E 404	Calcium Alginate		
E 405	Propylene Glycol Alginate	E 471	Mono- & diglycerides of fatty acids
E 406	Agar	E 472a	Acetic Acid Esters of mono- & diglycerides of fatty acids
E 407	Carrageenan		
E 410	Locust Bean Gum (Carob Gum)	E 472b	Lactic Acid Esters of mono- & diglycerides of fatty acids
E 412	Guar Gum		
E 413	Gum Tragacanth	E 472c	Citric Acid Esters of mono- & diglycerides of fatty acids
E 414	Gum Acacia (Gum Arabic)		
E 415	Xanthan Gum	E 472d	Tartaric Acid Esters of mono- & diglycerides of fatty acids
E 420	(i) Sorbitol (ii) Sorbitol syrup		
E 421	Mannitol	E 472e	Mono- & diacetyl Tartaric Esters of mono- & diglycerides of fatty acids
E 422	Glycerol (Glycerine)		
E 440a	Pectin		
E 440b	Amidated Pectin		
E 450a	(i) Disodium Dihydrogen Diphosphate	E 472f	Mixed Acetic & Tartaric Acid Esters of mono- & diglycerides of fatty acids
E 450a	(ii) Trisodium Diphosphate		
E 450a	(iii) Tetrasodium Diphosphate	E 473	Sucrose Esters of fatty acids
E 450a	(iv) Tetrapotassium Diphosphate	E 474	Sucroglycerides
E 450b	(i) Pentasodium Triphosphate	E 475	Polyglycerol Esters of fatty acids
E 450b	(ii) Pentapotassium Triphosphate	E 477	Propylene Glycol Esters of fatty acids
E 450c	(i) Sodium Polyphosphates	E 481	Sodium Stearoyl-2-lactylate
E 450c	(ii) Potassium Polyphosphates	E 482	Calcium Stearoyl-2-lactylate
		E 483	Stearyl Tartrate

INDEX